I0093134

SELF PUBLISHING SUCCESS

How to Write a Non-Fiction Book that Makes an Impact and Publish it Like a Pro

SHANDA TROFE

SELF-PUBLISHING SUCCESS

How to Write a Non-Fiction Book that Makes an Impact and Publish it Like a Pro

Copyright © 2022. Shanda Trofe. All Rights Reserved. No part of this publication may be reproduced, distributed, or transmitted in any form or by any means, including photocopying, recording, or other electronic or mechanical methods, without the prior written permission of the publisher, except in the case of brief quotations embodied in critical reviews and certain other noncommercial uses permitted by copyright law.

ISBN: 979-8-9857704-0-7 (Paperback)
ISBN: 979-8-9857704-4-5 (Hardcover)
ISBN: 979-8-9857704-2-1 (eBook)

Transcendent Publishing
PO Box 66202
St. Pete Beach, FL 33736
www.TranscendentPublishing.com

TRANSCENDEN
publishing

Printed in the United States of America.

Disclaimer: The author makes no guarantees concerning the level of success you may experience by following the advice and strategies contained in this book. This publication is meant as a source of valuable information for the reader; however, it is not meant as a substitute for direct expert assistance. If such level of assistance is required, the services of a competent professional should be sought.

"Before anything else, preparation is the key to success."

— Alexander Graham Bell

Contents

BONUS GIFT

Download your free
Self-Publishing Success Checklist

A three-part checklist to keep you on track
through the production, launch,
and post-launch marketing process.

Download it here:
www.shandatrofe.com/checklist

Introduction

One of the most valuable tools you can have for your brand or your business is a high-quality book.

A book, when done right, establishes credibility and authority. It showcases your expertise. More importantly, it makes a difference in the lives of your readers and inspires them to take action on the information you've provided.

So, you're probably wondering, what does it mean to write a book that makes an impact?

Have you ever read a book that changed your life in some way? Perhaps it taught you a new skill or served as a catalyst to move toward a dream or goal, thereby changing the trajectory of your future.

As an avid reader, I've had a handful of books that have done this for me, yet many more have missed the mark. Sure, I might have enjoyed them, but I cannot say they created a shift in my thinking and/or moved me to action. As a result, I've come to realize that there's a magic formula for a book that truly makes a meaningful, sustainable impact on its readers. I'll explain.

An example from my own bookshelf is Tim Ferriss's *The 4-Hour Work Week*. I found it in my twenties (I won't date myself but I'm referring to its first edition) while roaming through my local bookstore (yes, I'm further dating myself here), where it was featured on the front table of the hottest bestselling books. I'll never forget the moment the cover—a hammock strung between two palm trees—caught my eye. While the picture initially grabbed my attention (I was living in Michigan at the time and it happened to be the middle of a dreary winter), it was the title, *The 4-Hour Work Week*, that made a promise on a dream and left me intrigued enough to walk to the front of the store and buy it without hesitation or having even read the back cover.

From the first page, I was hooked, devouring every word, every story, every bit of advice. As Ferriss shared his adventures as a digital nomad, one where he wasn't tied to a nine-to-five job or a life of monotony, I could see my own future; he convinced me that I could have the kind of life I had, to that point, only dreamed of. He made me feel as if it were possible for me, too, and he also delivered valuable content and offered actionable steps I could take to create residual income and freedom in my life. Most importantly, he left me inspired to take action!

While I've never been able to adapt a four-hour work week into my own life, I do credit Ferriss and his revolutionary book as one that set my wheels in motion as an entrepreneur. Ironically, he helped me create a life and a business I love so much that I no longer desire a four-hour workweek. The point is, reading that book cover to cover was the pivotal moment in my life when I decided I would not be tied to corporate America, punch a clock, answer to a boss, or dedicate my life to building someone else's dream rather than my own. After a couple of failed attempts at various business ventures, I found, within a few short years, my true calling, and my self-publishing company, Transcendent Publishing, was born.

Over the past ten years, I've helped over five hundred aspiring authors realize their goal of becoming *bestselling* authors. Additionally, I've taught thousands of students from all over the globe through my online courses—something I can do from anywhere with a laptop and internet connection. So, you see, not only did that book make an impact on me, it inadvertently impacted thousands of others through my teaching, coaching, courses, books, and done-for-you service.

That's the type of book that makes a difference, and that's the kind of book I'm inspiring *you* to write for your audience.

You may be thinking that you don't have anything revolutionary to share. I hear these same self-doubts arise from aspiring authors all the time…

This has all been done before; what makes my book any different from what's already out there?

And furthermore, who's going to care?

Who am I to write a book, anyway?

First, let me just say that there is always a unique way to share your knowledge with the world. Nobody will have your same insights, experiences, stories, or share your message quite like you.

There are thousands upon thousands of books on self-publishing, but I didn't bat an eye when it came time to write this book. Why? Because my goal is to create something that makes a ripple in this world, moves you to think differently and, hopefully, to take that inspired action I mentioned earlier. Do I expect this book to be revolutionary or groundbreaking? Probably not, though one can hope. What I can do is write on a topic I'm both passionate and knowledgeable about while delivering the content in a way that empowers my readers and offers measurable results.

If you read my book *Authorpreneur: How to Build an Empire and Become the AUTHORity in Your Business*, then you already know I'm a big fan of acronyms. If you haven't read it yet, I won't spoil it for you; however, I will share that at the end I used the acronym E.M.P.I.R.E to help my readers remember the main takeaways from the content. That's why it only seemed fitting that for this book, with its subtitle *How to Write a Non-Fiction Book that Makes an Impact and Publish it Like a Pro*, I'd follow in my previous footsteps and create an acronym for you to keep in mind as you write your own book.

That Acronym is I.M.P.A.C.T.

I - **Inspire** your readers. As mentioned in my example above, *The 4-Hour Work Week* caused a shift in my perspective and opened my mind to what was truly possible for me. And, while my first few attempts at entrepreneurship did not meet with success, I was ultimately able to find my passion and my purpose, which led to the life I live today. One that I created because Mr. Ferris was able to inspire me, through his words, to take action.

M - **Measurable** results. Offer your readers an outcome they can measure, and they will see your book as a success. By the end of your book your reader should be able to take action on what you've shared by applying it in his or her own life and get a tangible result. That result is evidence to your reader that what you taught was invaluable and practical. This is key if you expect your reader to trust you or continue the journey with you.

P - **Passionate** topic. One of my all-time favorite quotes is by Bishop T.D. Jakes. He says, "If you can't figure out your purpose, figure out your passion. For your passion will lead you right into your purpose." This rang true for me when I was struggling to find my own path in life. I believe we all have a message to share and a reason for being here. I believe we've endured the experiences we've had throughout our lives because we are meant to share our stories and guide others on a similar path. That passion to help others get their messages out in the world led me to my career as a book coach and self-publishing guide, and that has indirectly led this book to you. When you can write on something you're both passionate and knowledgeable about, you'll have a winner.

A – **Authority**-building. Writing your book will establish you as an expert in your niche and open doors to new opportunities. The sky's the limit once you become a published author, especially a bestselling author, which I'll teach you how to do later in the book.

C – **Credibility**-lending. Do you desire to speak on stage, teach, coach, or simply grow your business? Writing a high-quality book that makes an impact is one of the fastest ways to establish credibility in your business. It's also a great way to turn your readers into clients, which is the ultimate goal. Once you're a bestselling author with a high-quality book, you'll find it's easier to charge a premium for your services such as high-ticket coaching, should you desire to take that path, or get booked for high-paying speaking gigs. At the very least, you'll receive invitations to speak on podcast interviews, in summits, as a guest contributor, and more.

T - **Teach** and offer action steps. Your book should be a nice balance of teaching and sharing of experiences from your own life or those of others. Don't have any clients yet? Reference experiences of public figures or well-known people (just be sure to get the details accurate). The point is, people learn best through stories, so back up each concept you introduce with an example to paint the picture and further drive home your intended takeaway. In a well-written book, a reader will not only learn something new, they will be left with a clear plan of action for applying your concepts to their own lives. And if you've done things right, they'll feel a deep connection to you and want more from you, the expert.

In the pages ahead, I'm going to share how you can write and self-publish a high-quality book that meets all the components of I.M.P.AC.T. and ultimately turns your readers into clients or lifelong fans. Ready to get started?

Let's begin...

CHAPTER 1

Why Self-Publishing is a Great Option for Your Business

There's never been a better time in history to become an authorpreneur and embrace the world of self-publishing.

The global pandemic of 2020 changed the publishing industry dramatically. Traditional publishers, who rely heavily on bookstore sales, were hit hard with the global shutdowns of retail businesses. Some stores reported to the American Booksellers Association that their sales were down at least 40%[1]. Consumers turned more than ever to online retailers such as Amazon to supply their books. Amazon is the biggest force in book sales in the U.S. market today, accounting for over 90 percent of e-books and audiobooks, and around 42 to 45% of print sales[2].

---

[1] https://www.nytimes.com/2020/12/29/books/book-publishing-2020.html
[2] https://selfpublishingadvice.org/facts-and-figures-about-self-publishing-the-impact-and-influence-of-indie-authors/

Additionally, e-book and audiobook sales rose as more and more readers embraced the instant access of these formats as the new norm, with e-book sales up by 22% in 2020, while audiobook sales increased by 39%[3]. Still, print book sales have increased 13.2% between 2020 and 2021[4], so don't discount the power of publishing your book in print just yet.

The publishing industry generates around $26 billion in revenue in the United States every year[5]. As of 2020, 1.7 million new books were self-published in the U.S. That's an increase of 264% within the past five years and makes up 43% of the total new books published[6], so it's easy to see why this is a great time to jump into the indie world of self-publishing.

Book publishing is not the only thing that has changed over the past couple of years. People turned, more than ever, to virtual courses for learning, coaches and masterminds for support, and social media to engage with each other. Digital education and eLearning industries are expected to grow to $243 billion by 2022[7]. In a time when we may be socially distancing in public, the internet provides us with that much-needed connection to our friends, family, favorite authors, mentors, and society as a whole.

What does this mean for you as an author? It's the best time to begin building your author empire. Yes, the world has now opened

---

[3] https://publishingperspectives.com/2021/06/audio-publishers-association-12-percent-audiobook-revenue-growth-in-2020-covid19/

[4] https://www.vox.com/culture/22687960/book-shortage-paper-ink-printing-labor-explained

[5] https://www.statista.com/statistics/271931/revenue-of-the-us-book-publishing-industry/

[6] https://www.zippia.com/advice/us-book-industry-statistics/

[7] https://www.statista.com/topics/3115/e-learning-and-digital-education/

back up, but that doesn't mean things will ever go back entirely to the way they were. We have now grown used to consuming our books, education, and entertainment at a digital level, and that's likely here to stay.

This means it's the ideal time to write your book, publish it in multiple formats including print, e-book and audio, and then expand upon your message through other offerings to grow your business.

Let's Start with the Paperback

Let's say that you buy your wholesale copies directly from the printer, and then you resell those copies at the retail rate at your live events, workshops, speaking engagements, on your website or via social media. Well, because you ordered those copies directly from the printer at wholesale, you'll retain the difference in profits from your retail rate.

For instance, if you have a standard 6x9, two-hundred-page book with black and white interior (color interior will drive up the price of printing and eat into your profits, so usually we try to stick to black and white when we can), you're going to pay approximately $3 to $4 per copy, depending on a few variables.

For the sake of this example, let's say your book retails for $16.99. That means after you take into account the cost to ship your wholesale copies to you, you get to keep approximately $10 to $11 per copy from sales you make by your own efforts. This is a great option for speakers, coaches, course creators, online marketers, and entrepreneurs who will then sell their books on their websites or at live events.

Now, you may be wondering, *If my paperback sells on Amazon, wouldn't I make the same profit?* The answer is no. When someone goes to Amazon to purchase your book, Amazon fills that order and ships it directly to them—and passes the distribution costs to you. After those costs, you get paid a royalty on the sale, typically around 60% for a paperback. We'll get into those details a bit later; just know that royalty is far greater than you would receive from traditional publishers, who pay their authors 8 to 15% royalties by industry standard.

With self-publishing, you're cutting out the middleman and you don't have to share a percentage of your royalties with a publisher. I don't know about you, but I'd rather retain 60% of my royalties than 15%!

For online sales, your book distributor will disburse your royalties monthly (direct deposited into your bank account); keep in mind, though, that most pay on a sixty-day lag, so you won't see your first royalty payment for a couple of months post-publication.

Don't get me wrong, you'll definitely want to make your book available via online retailers as well. Right now I'm just explaining the difference between selling it yourself from your own inventory of wholesale copies, or receiving a royalty from your distributors, such as Kindle Direct Publishing (KDP) or IngramSpark for online sales, which are the two I prefer and recommend to my clients.

So you see, self-publishing a book can be highly lucrative, especially when you sell your paperbacks through your own efforts at events, on your website, or through a book funnel, which I'll touch on later.

Now, for the E-book

When you distribute your e-book with KDP, and price it between $2.99 and $9.99, you'll retain 70% of the royalties. Above or below that price range, you'll receive 35% of the sale. Now you may be wondering, *Why would I price my e-book out of the 70% royalty range?* We will typically drop the price of the e-book to $.99 during the launch to bestseller, or while hosting quarterly promotions. Yes, dropping your e-book to $.99 will only earn you 35% of the sale, but you'll usually get a higher number of downloads at that price point, especially when you are driving traffic to the e-book with paid features from book promoters or Amazon ads. Therefore, the temporary price drop is a strategic and sometimes necessary move.

This is also beneficial if you have a way to collect contact information from your readers, for example, by offering a free bonus gift inside your book that they must opt-in to your mailing list to receive. Thus, each quarterly promotion is an opportunity to grow your mailing list and potentially gain new clients for your business or backend offer. As the name suggests, the backend offer is what you present to the reader at the end of the book so they may continue the journey with you, for example, by purchasing one of your higher-ticket products or services.

As you can see, the e-book edition can be a powerful tool for your business, to attract new readers, grow your mailing list, and ultimately turn readers into clients. They also provide instant gratification, with live links inside that allow your readers to sign up for your mailing list or visit your website with a simple click, then go back to reading your impactful words.

Also, e-books sold 191 million units in 2020[8], with *Amazon's share of the e-book market at 68%*[9] so you don't want to miss out on this powerful way to deliver your content and reach your readers.

Finally, Let's Talk Audiobooks

Audiobooks are one of the fastest-growing sectors of the publishing industry. The global audiobook market, which was valued at $4 billion in 2020, is estimated by industry experts to grow to $20 billion by 2030[10]. This makes sense, for as mentioned earlier in the chapter people are consuming their information differently nowadays, and for many, that means listening to books in audio format while doing other things such as driving, cleaning the house, exercising, or doing yardwork. So, in my opinion, if you don't put your book in audio format, you're leaving money on the table.

It's been my experience that many authors think it's too large of an undertaking to produce their books in audio format, so they skip this step altogether. However, it can be quite easy and cost-effective if you opt to hire a narrator instead of narrating the book yourself. With Audible's Audiobook Creation Exchange (ACX), you can find and hire a narrator in the voice of your choosing, and ACX will take care of the contract and the disbursing of royalties and payments.

When you find a narrator you like, you can either pay them upfront for their recording hours (in which case you'll retain the net royalties),

---

[8] https://www.zippia.com/advice/us-book-industry-statistics/

[9] https://about.ebooks.com/ebook-industry-news-feed/

[10] https://www.financialexpress.com/brandwagon/hear-we-grow-audiobooks-witnesses-a-rise-as-more-users-join-the-bandwagon/2325233/

or sometimes negotiate to pay nothing upfront in exchange for a split of the royalties. That is what I did with the audiobook for *Authorpreneur* and, except for a small fee to have my cover designer size the cover to ACX's guidelines, I paid nothing out of pocket.

If I had decided to instead pay my narrator upfront, it would have cost me approximately $1,500, as ACX estimated my 180-page book to be five hours in audiobook format, and that particular narrator charged $300 per hour.

Instead, I let the narrator know that I had a solid marketing plan in place for the book and offered to split my royalties with her if she'd narrate it for no upfront fees, and she agreed. ACX compiled our agreement and they split and disburse the royalties each month on our behalf.

Since I also opted into Audible's exclusivity plan, meaning I agreed not to sell my audiobook elsewhere, we split a 40% royalty cut each month, or 20% each. (If you do not opt into their exclusivity program, you'll receive 25% of the royalties.) For me, offering exclusivity was a no-brainer, because with their program my audiobook is for sale on Audible, Amazon and iTunes. However, I have some clients who utilize their audiobooks for a book funnel, therefore, they do not opt in for exclusivity so they can also offer the audio version of their book as an upsell inside that funnel.

As you can see, there are benefits to offering exclusivity for 40% of the royalties, or opting out and retaining 25%. What you choose is up to you, just don't miss out on revenue because of preconceived notions about the additional steps needed to produce an audiobook, or the value of having one.

Findaway Voices is another popular platform in the audiobook industry. It enables authors to distribute audiobooks across a diverse range of retailers, including Spotify and Google Play. If you plan to distribute your audiobook with Findaway Voices in addition to ACX, you will not be able to offer ACX exclusivity (and vice versa), so be sure to keep that in mind when uploading your audiobook and selecting distribution options.

Oftentimes, authors say to me: "I don't listen to audiobooks, so I don't see the point"; or "I prefer paperbacks over e-books, so I don't really care about publishing my book in digital format." That's the worst mistake you can make if you want to earn a sizable income with your book and get it into the most hands. Don't let your personal preferences for consuming content dictate the formats in which you distribute it. People like to consume content differently, so let the statistics speak for themselves and don't leave money on the table.

CHAPTER 2

Write with the End Goal in Mind (and set yourself up for long-term success)

One of the first things I have my clients do when they set out to write a book is establish their "why" for writing that book in the first place.

There are many reasons why someone might decide to write a book. Usually, though, it's because they want to help others through their message—an admirable reason that should not be discounted. I believe those of us who are called to write do so because we want to be of service in some way; otherwise, we wouldn't run the risk of putting our vulnerable selves out in a world that can sometimes be harsh and judgmental.

A need outside of yourself, such as the desire to inspire, teach and help others, should always be the primary reason for writing a book. It's what will keep your engine running to make it to the finish line on those hard writing days when you want to give up (yes, we all have them). In these times, as you place your fingers on the keyboard or grip the pen, it's helpful to hold in your mind the person who can most benefit from your message and write for him or her, first and foremost.

Take a moment to think about your "why" for writing your book. I'd also encourage you to take out a sheet of paper or journal and write out your why. Keep it somewhere handy where you can reference it often, as it will serve as a powerful reminder in those tough moments when you question why you even started your writing journey.

Now that we've established your primary reason, I'd like you to discover your secondary reason, as this will determine how you deliver your content—keeping your ultimate end goal in mind while doing so—and how you'll earn income from your book. Here's a hint: If you're a savvy authorpreneur, it will come from backend sales.

To explain what I mean, here are my primary and secondary reasons for writing this book:

I started self-publishing back in 2012. It was a time when I was being called to find my life purpose and really figure out what I was put on this earth to do. I knew I was passionate about books, writing, and was enamored with authors. That was something I could trace back to childhood, when I would devour books and dream of someday writing some of my own. However, throughout my teens and twenties I had put those dreams aside as I sought to find my bearings in this world. It wasn't until I was in my thirties that I decided to return to college, this time to study Creative Writing and English. I remember having no plan of action for what I would do with that degree, if I even got one. That was never really my goal. I only set out to finally pursue my dream to write and bring some joy and creativity to my life.

I recall people often asking me why I was enrolled in a writing program, and some even offered their unsolicited opinion that I was wasting my time and would never make any real money as a writer. But at the time, it didn't matter. I was just following my passion, probably for the first time in my life, and for me, that meant working my way through a writing program. At the same time, I was also on a spiritual journey of self-discovery and personal development.

Two years into the writing program, I got an inspired idea. I wanted to create a free platform where writers, or and anyone with messages to share, could come together and publish their essays, blog posts, articles, passages, poems, prayers, etc. online. Thus, my free membership community Spiritual Writers Network was formed.

One month later, I had over 1,000 registered writers sharing their daily writing on the website, which quickly grew to over 3,000 members. I knew I was onto something, and from there my desire to help our members on a larger scale emerged.

I had just self-published my first e-book, which was a huge learning experience filled with trial and error as I navigated my way through the process. That's when I got an idea to start offering writing contests via Spiritual Writers Network, and then turn those entries into multi-author compilation-style books so that our members could also become published authors, further broadening the stage for them. I ran the contests quarterly and helped hundreds of our writers get published, and that quickly evolved into helping many of those same authors self-publish their own solo books. That is how my publishing company came to be.

Over that time, and in working with so many authors, I noticed patterns begin to emerge. I noticed some authors would try to rush the process and skimp on some of the important components that make up a high-quality book. This resulted in a product they were not proud of and therefore unwilling to share with the world. I also noticed some authors thought they could just upload a manuscript and DIY cover to Amazon and hit publish, without a proper launch or marketing plan in place. Then, when their book got lost in the vast ocean that is Amazon (as it inevitably will without a proper launch and strategic plan) they thought their book was a failure, which deflated their confidence and, in many cases, their motivation to continue writing.

Though this genuinely hurt my heart to witness, I came to realize that it was through watching these experiences unfold that my own "why" began to develop. This is when I started offering online courses, group coaching programs, private author coaching, my done-for-you self-publishing services, and bestseller book launches. It became my life's work to ensure that aspiring authors were set up for success. This meant educating them on how to build a solid author platform, how to self-publish a high-quality book, and to set up a proper launch that earns their book plenty of reviews and ignites Amazon's algorithm to enhance their book's searchability. This is also the reason I wrote the first edition of *Authorpreneur* back in 2016.

The best part? Through my desire to serve my readers and clients, I've made multiple six figures on my backend sales since publishing *Authorpreneur*. I did that by creating the services that my readers needed, beyond the book. I knew I wasn't going to get rich on my royalties alone, even though that book has sold quite well. It's everything I created *after* the book was published, with the book at the foundation of it all, that brings in the real income in my business.

You see, my primary why for writing that book, as well as this one, and all the coaching and teaching I've done in between, is that I genuinely want to help authors succeed.

Now, let's explore my secondary why, which is to grow and benefit my business while fulfilling my primary why. And that's okay! There's nothing wrong with writing a book to benefit your own life as well as your readers.

I believe many of us are taught at a young age that doing something for ourselves is selfish and ego-based. But here's the thing: it isn't selfish to create a book for your business so that you establish credibility. That credibility will lead to more readers trusting you and finding your backend offers (which we'll get to in just a moment). In other words, it will help you convert your readers into clients, and if you are writing a book for your business, that's the ultimate goal.

Nor is it selfish to write a book that offers incredible value on its own but also offers a product or service at the end. This is simply a way for your readers to delve deeper and take your concepts or teaching to the next level. The key is to ensure that your book can stand on its own and positively impact the reader, whether or not they choose to continue working with you.

If you believe in your work and you know there are people out there who can benefit from what you have to offer, then it's not selfish to want to earn income from your books so that you can create more time and freedom in your life. The more income and freedom you can generate, the more time you can spend writing and teaching, and that will only help you impact more lives in the long run! I speak from experience, and I encourage you to remember those people the next time you question your motivation.

Now that we've gotten that out of the way, let's look at some of the common secondary reasons for writing a book:

- To establish authority and credibility by positioning yourself as an expert in your niche ... *so you can impact more lives...*
- To turn your readers into clients and grow your business ... *so you can impact more lives...*
- To funnel your readers into your other offers such as a done-for-you service, high-level coaching program, mastermind, membership site, online course, or other books you've published (or will publish in the future) ... *so you can impact more lives...*
- To become a speaker or increase your speaking fees so you can get on more stages, podcasts, and summits ... *and impact more lives!*

You see, your secondary reason is ancillary and in support of your primary reason. Again, the primary reason should always be your why, and I believe if you first and foremost set out to help others from a place of service, the entire Universe will conspire to help you meet success.

Let's take a moment to think about your secondary reason for writing your book. And, just as you did with the primary reason, grab a sheet of paper and write out your secondary why. This step is important, so don't skip it.

When you think about your life a year or two from now, how is your book supporting you? How has your life changed since becoming a published author? Perhaps you are teaching workshops and/or online courses, speaking, or hosting a mastermind. As you work through the remaining chapters of this book, it will be important to keep these goals in mind, because how you structure your book and deliver your message will depend on what your end goal is and who you want to serve.

Start with the end goal in mind, and you will write a book that speaks to your target audience or ideal reader (who is also your ideal client). Take some time to flesh out your ideal reader/client as well. Know exactly who you want to attract through your message, what their pain points are, as well as their goals and dreams, because that's who you want to have at the forefront of your mind when you write your book. You'll want to overcome their objections, squash their fears, and deliver on your promise, which ultimately is the answer to their problem.

CHAPTER 3

Writing and Structuring
Your Impactful Book

Now it's time to get started writing, but where to begin?

It's possible your book is already written and you've purchased this book to learn the self-publishing piece; if that's the case, I'd encourage you to read through this chapter anyway and use it as a checklist to ensure you've structured your book in a way that is going to speak to your ideal reader and overcome their objections. This way, as mentioned, when they get to the end of your book you will have established yourself as an expert, gained their trust, delivered value, and they will be ready to continue engaging with you through whatever else you have to offer. At the very least, they'll have joined your mailing list where they'll receive even more value, and will hopefully become a client over time.

For the sake of this chapter, I'm going to assume you are starting at the beginning. You have an idea for a book, likely one that's been gnawing at you for some time, and you're ready to get that idea out of your heart and mind and onto paper. Maybe you already have a business and you want to share your expertise through a book that will lend you credibility, or you have an idea for a business and you know that becoming an author is a great way to build authority and attract new clients.

But I Don't Have the Time

Before we get into the *how*, let's get you into the proper mindset to write your book. I know what you're probably thinking: *I've been wanting to write a book, but I just don't have the time.* I know this because it's the number one objection I hear from aspiring authors each and every day. Here's the thing: the timing will never be *just right.* There will always be some reason to delay the process, because, let's face it, life gets in the way *when* we allow it to.

People make time for things that are important to them, and you will too. But first you have to decide with one hundred percent certainty that you're ready to do this, and you have to *create* the time in your schedule. You do that by developing a plan of action and sticking to it. By making sacrifices in your schedule to carve out time for writing. By becoming so consumed by your book that you power through to the finish line. And I'm going to be honest with you and tell you, it won't always be easy. There will be days when you want to quit, and, if you aren't careful, you'll put your book on the back burner midway through. I'm also going to tell you that once you do that, it's incredibly hard to get started again.

So here's my recommendation: Decide that this is what you want to do, and just do it. Offer yourself a short period of time to complete the first draft, with a concrete deadline, and work diligently toward that goal until it's completed. Don't allow yourself to put the project aside midway through. Decide before you even begin that this is your number one priority and see it through to completion.

Also, don't offer yourself a year to finish the first draft. The longer you allow yourself, the more likely you are to only work on it when you are inspired, and that could easily stretch into two, three or even more years. The world needs your wisdom and all that you have to offer, and if you're writing a book for your business, let's face it, you need that book out sooner rather than later.

Finding Your Target Daily Word Count

The first step in finding your target daily word count is setting a goal for the final word count of your manuscript.

If you are creating a product for your business, it's likely that you are setting out to write a non-fiction book, so between 30,000-50,000 words is a good target to aim for. I like to aim for 40,000 words, and that's what I recommend to my clients. You may go over or fall a bit short, and that is fine.

For example, I estimated my final word count for this book at 40,000 before I began, and wound up with a first draft of 39,689 words. I stayed true to my goal. Once finished with my final draft, I was just over 35,000 words since my editor cut a bit of redundancy along with an unnecessary chapter, but that word count is also within range. That's the importance of a good editor, by the way. Don't be afraid to cut your word count to be more concise. Your readers will appreciate you cutting the "fluff" and saving time by staying true to the point.

You could even look at the page count and thickness of this book and use that as a gauge for the desired length of your own book. Keep in mind, this won't be an exact measurement because all books vary depending on design, trim size, font style and size, spacing, etc., but it will at least give you an idea of what a 35,000-word book looks like.

For my clients, I've published non-fiction books anywhere from 100 to 480 pages, so it is really up to you. That said, on average a book of 150 to 200 pages is ideal for a non-fiction business book, so that means 40,000 words is an ideal goal.

Now that you have a goal for your final word count, you can easily set a goal for your target daily word count; first, though, you will need to set a deadline for your first draft. I will ask you to write your first draft in a condensed block of time, and *then* spend a decent amount of time revising, editing and crafting the final product. The reason is this: If you set out to write your first draft within a shorter time frame, you are less likely to stop the flow of creativity each day by going back and editing as you write. When you write freely, you unlock the flow and silence the ego—that voice that second-guesses your word choices and tells you your last line was awful and you need to rewrite it. However, when you break that creative flow it takes approximately twenty minutes to get back into it—time you cannot afford to waste if, like me, you only set aside an hour or two each day to write.

Organizing the process into phases will help you write unencumbered each day, knowing that there will be plenty of time for revision in the next draft. In turn, you will write your first draft much faster and it will likely flow more easily.

Again, it's up to you how much time you want to allow yourself to write, but for a non-fiction book I like to set a goal of ninety days from start to completion date. This book is the foundation for your business, and although it shouldn't be rushed (you want to put out a high-quality product), you shouldn't give yourself too much time to write the manuscript. The goal is to get the book done so you start reaping the benefits of authorship, so, again, I would urge you to set a shorter (but realistic) time frame and work diligently toward it each day. This will keep the momentum going for your project, increasing your probability of achieving success much faster.

Defining Your Avatar/Ideal Reader

Now that you have a timeline and clear plan of action for when and how you'll complete your book, it's time to get crystal clear on *who* you're writing to. I touched on this earlier, but this is a critically important step and deserves to be discussed in more detail. At this point you may be thinking, *But my book doesn't only help one type of person. It could help this audience, and that audience too,* and so on. I hear this all the time from my clients, and I get it. There will always be more than one audience who can benefit from a book. However, the idea here is to focus on one reader as you write, and here's a hint: that reader should also be your dream client.

So take some time to think about your dream client for a moment. If you already have a business, it may be a client you've worked with in the past. You know the one—they know instantly that they want to work with you, they pay in full, do everything you ask of them, and are easily coachable and eager to learn. They go on to become long-term clients by jumping on everything you offer in the future, and singing your praises to anyone and everyone who will listen.

If you don't yet have a business, use your imagination.

Begin by making a list of everything your ideal client encompasses. Start simple with the demographics: gender, age, location, income, education level, marital status, occupation, and number of children.

Next, you're going to want to dig a bit deeper. This is where you'll think about their goals and dreams, and what keeps them up at night. What do they hope to achieve? What are their long-term goals, and what short-term goals might they need to accomplish to get there?

Once you've figured that out, explore what might be holding them back. What are their obstacles, both internal and external? By internal, I mean, what within them stops them from moving forward? Is it fear, self-doubt, lack of knowledge, perhaps? Conversely, what external factors hinder their progress? Lack of time, support from family, or income to fund their dreams?

What have they already tried in the past that hasn't worked? What misconceptions might they have about your niche or process?

Here's a hint: Your ideal client is usually a lot like you, or rather who you were before you learned what you're going to share inside your book. So think back to the person you used to be, when you were in your ideal client's shoes, and do this exercise through the lens of their eyes.

Success Tip: If you already have a client base established, survey them. The best way to figure out the answers to these questions is not to guess but rather go directly to the source and ask. If you don't have a client base of your own, consider creating a Facebook group around your topic or area of expertise and ask three qualifying questions for new members upon approval. You can add these questions under the settings tab.

For my Facebook group, Self-Publishing Success, I ask these three questions for new members requesting approval:

1. What's your #1 goal when it comes to writing, publishing, or book marketing?
2. What holds you back from reaching that goal?
3. Would you like to receive free self-publishing tips to your inbox? If so, drop your email address below to join my mailing list and receive a free copy of my *Self-Publishing Success Checklist.*

Now, each time a new member joins my Facebook group, I learn my ideal client/readers' goals and objections. I store that info on a spreadsheet so I can review it as needed, such as when it's time to create new content for my group, or write a new book such as this one.

I also send out an annual survey to my mailing list each year with additional questions so they have the opportunity to offer more feedback. This way, I feel I know my audience well and can create and publish content based on their needs instead of what I *think* they need or want to know. Plus, I can also use the verbiage from their responses in my future marketing efforts so my offer really speaks to their desires and pain points.

For instance, as mentioned earlier, one obstacle I hear from almost everyone who wants to write a book is the demand on their time. Because, let's face it, we are all busy. Who really has the time to write a book? And because I know this is the number one objection from my audience, I know that I have to overcome that objection every time I offer a new book-writing course or program. After all, if my avatar doesn't believe she can find the time to write a book, then there is no use in teaching her how. So we always begin as I did at the beginning of this chapter—by explaining how she can create a structure and schedule for her writing journey. See what I did there?

Now that you know who you're writing to and what potential obstacles they may need to overcome, you have a clear avatar to hold in your mind's eye as you write.

Brainstorming Your Book Idea

Brainstorming—or writing freely whatever thoughts and words come to mind—is a great tool to help you flesh out any creative project, including your book. While the ideas that come during this process might, at first, not make much sense, they can be invaluable in helping define your content and spark even more inspiration. Therefore, during your brainstorming session, be mindful not to question what comes up. You're opening up potential channels and possibilities. Stopping to second-guess yourself at this stage stunts idea generation and limits creativity.

Some prefer a simple listing technique while others like the "bubbles and branches" technique: the main topic in the center of the paper, and each new idea branching off into a new bubble, with fresh insights branching off each as they arise.

Even if you have a clear vision of how your book will develop, it might be a good idea to work through this exercise to see if any new insights arise.

For example, when you later go back and review your brainstorming session, you may begin to see how certain topics could become potential chapters, and how sub-topics might become subheadings within those chapters.

If you are toying with a few book ideas and are unsure of which to begin first, I would highly encourage you to work through the brainstorming exercise for each of your book ideas individually. Then you'll know which session flowed most freely, got you most excited, and sparked enough ideas for an entire book.

Creating a Roadmap for Your Book-Writing Journey

Now that you've completed your brainstorming session, take the ideas you've collected to create a loose outline for your book.

Outlines are a matter of personal choice for each writer. Some writers are organized and follow their outline rigorously, while others don't like to be as structured and want to see where the journey takes them. I like to start with a basic outline before I begin a book yet remain open to inspiration when the book decides to take off in a new direction. Whatever your preference, it's nice to have a roadmap to aid in organizing your thoughts and incorporating the ideas from your brainstorming session.

First, look at the results from your brainstorming session. You can probably see how certain topics are clustered together to form a potential chapter. For now, start separating your ideas by chapter, without thinking of a logical order. You may want to use index cards for this, with each chapter topic at the top of the card with three to five bullet points listed on what you will include within that chapter.

Once you have as many chapters as you can think of, add a few bullets for your Introduction, Conclusion, and About the Author page. That's a good start for now; later you can add the Dedication, Acknowledgments, Endorsements, Appendixes (optional), Bonus Gift, and a strong Call-to-Action page to drive traffic to your other products and services.

Your outline will become a "to-do list" for your book, and you can fill in the blanks out of order if you choose. There is no right or wrong, and yours will differ depending on the genre or form in which you have decided to write, so I'm not going to put too much emphasis on how to create an outline because I don't want you to get inside your head about whether or not you're doing it right. It's simply an exercise to help organize your thoughts and come up with chapter ideas along with a few bullet points for each, so that you can reference your notes as needed once you begin writing.

As valuable as the outline is, the mere notion of creating it can often be intimidating to aspiring authors; in fact, this is where many become overwhelmed and abandon the project. For that reason, I am going to keep this task as simple as possible. Try not to overthink it; remember, you don't need to have everything figured out before you begin. Again, the outline is an excellent guidance tool, but how detailed you make it and how often you refer to it during the writing process is a personal choice.

Writing a Compelling Introduction

For non-fiction, I usually recommend that you open your book with an introduction. This sets the tone for what's to come, and it's also where many readers will decide if they are going to invest in your book and take this journey with you.

Your introduction needs to inform yet intrigue your reader. Also, keep in mind that they may not know who you are or why they should listen to you, so it's important that you touch on that as well (this goes to the credibility-building I mentioned earlier). I'm not saying to include your full bio in your introduction, but you'll want to slide in a few sentences, or even a paragraph, about what you do (title/experience), who you serve (avatar), and how much experience you have, if any. The point is, don't wait until the "About the Author" section, usually found at the back of the book, to reveal how and why you're knowledgeable on your topic.

The introduction should also include what inspired you to write your book, so this is an opportunity to open up and share more about yourself and your own journey. This is usually what got you from where you were (and where your reader likely is now) to where you are now (your avatar's ultimate goal).

It should also be motivating and end strong so that it leaves your reader inspired to turn the page (or "Buy Now" online) and dive in.

With Amazon's "Look Inside" feature, readers can view the first 10% of a book before they purchase. This allows them to get a taste of your writing style, your message, and what's to come. Depending on the length of your book and how you structure your front matter, this will usually contain your introduction, so be sure it's compelling.

This is also why I don't recommend that you fill the front of your book with components that could instead go at the back, such as the Acknowledgments and About the Author sections.

So, how does one craft a compelling introduction? I've found one of the best ways to begin is with a journaling session to flesh out your "why" for writing the book. So grab a notebook or journal, find a quiet space where you'll be able to work through this exercise uninterrupted, and begin journaling your responses to these questions:

- What's my #1 reason/goal for writing this book?
- What inspired me to write this book in the first place?
- Who do I hope to help? Define your ideal audience in a nutshell.
- What benefits will I offer my reader? In other words, what objections will I overcome?
- Why am I credible and why should they listen to me?
- What experience do I have around this topic that my reader can benefit from?
- What can I share about my own journey that led me to discover what I'm sharing in this book?

- How can I close out my introduction and leave them inspired to dive into the content? What would I have needed to hear back when I was in this reader's shoes to let me know I can take this journey too, and what's the best way to explain how this book is going to guide them along the way?
- What is my bold promise to my reader?

Success Tip: Don't be afraid to share something vulnerable, as this will connect your reader to you on a deeper level and establish trust from the start.

Once you've journaled on those answers, you should have enough content to write an introduction that draws your reader in and makes them want more.

How to Structure a Strong Chapter

I often get asked how long a chapter should be. That answer varies considerably, depending on your projected word count and the number of chapters you'll include in your book. If you're writing a 40,000-word book, your chapters may be slightly longer than if you were writing a short book of 25,000 words, for instance.

I always recommend that a chapter should begin and end where it feels complete to the author. If you've noticed, some chapters in this book are longer than others, and that's okay. I'm not going to add fluff and filler to a chapter just to reach a certain word count. Once I've explained my main point and provided a story or an example to back up my claim, the chapter ends. For some of the chapters I had a lot more to include, such as this chapter on writing and structuring your impactful book, which is one of the longest in the book.

I will say this: be wary of making your chapters too long. There is such a thing as "reader fatigue," and it can affect the reader's experience of the book. My chapters typically range from 1,500 to 3,000 words. If a chapter begins to stretch beyond 3,000 words, you might consider breaking it into two chapters.

Next, what should you include in your chapters? For a non-fiction book, each chapter should have a theme or main topic. You'll want to open the chapter by introducing that topic, then follow up with a story or example that backs up that claim and further explains it to your reader. Readers like to learn by example and through stories that contextualize what you're teaching and help them make sense of it.

Subsections—or concepts that fall under the main topic—can also be a very useful tool in structuring your chapter, especially if it is a lengthier one and contains a lot of information. Take this chapter, for example: *How to Write and Structure Your Impactful Book*. I have many subtopics that fall under the umbrella of this chapter, so I broke those up under the following subheadings:

- Overcoming the Objection of Time
- Defining Your Ideal Reader
- Brainstorming Your Book Idea
- Creating a Loose Outline

- Writing a Compelling Introduction
- How to Structure a Strong Chapter
- The Inspired Close
- Continue the Journey

Like I said, this is one of my longer chapters in the book, and having these subtopics, all of which fall under the main topic of writing and structuring your book, makes it more easily digestible for the reader. For the same reason, it's also a good idea to think about any exercises, tools, or processes you might include. This is also why I ask you to come up with a few bullet points of things you'll cover in each chapter while creating your loose outline.

Finally, when you close out each chapter you may want to summarize your main takeaway(s), then segue into the next chapter so your reader wants to continue reading and doesn't close the book.

The Inspired Close

You've written an impactful book, and now it must come to an end. But how? With a strong closing chapter, that's how.

Before you write your closing, it's a good time to reflect on what you delivered as content in your book, and what the number one thing you hope your reader took away from it. Think back on your theme and main topic for your book, and the final result you are hoping your reader will achieve from what you have to offer.

Hint: Your main takeaway is usually what you promised in your subtitle! Here's an example:

For this book, my main topic is self-publishing. My goal is to help you meet success on your self-publishing journey by writing an impactful, high-quality book and then self-publish it properly without making unnecessary mistakes along the way. Hence my subtitle: *How to Write a Nonfiction Book that Makes an Impact and Publish it Like a Pro.* Therefore, before I close out this book, I'll ask myself: Does my book deliver on that promise? Did I stay true to that content, and if so, what closing message would I like to deliver to my reader to summarize my main goal?

I want you to get results, so when I close out this book I'll remind you to follow the steps, invest in your book's production, remind you not to rush the important steps of that production process, and leave you inspired to get started.

When it's time for you to wrap up your book, you'll want to do the same. I can't tell you how many authors send me their manuscript for review because they believe it's complete, but the book abruptly ends after their last chapter, without a strong close. Do this and you're missing out on an incredible opportunity to connect with your reader one last time before they close the book forever.

Remember, your goal is to get your readers results, so just as the opening of your book must be a compelling "hook," the close must be a strong summary of your takeaway that inspires them to act on the processes and tips you've shared throughout—and continue the journey with you as a client.

Speaking of which, a strong close will segue nicely into your back of the book offer…

Continue the Journey

If your reader made it to the end of your book, they likely enjoyed the content and want more of what you have to offer. Think about the last book you enjoyed. The rest of the world melted away as you read it, and you were likely bummed when it came to a close. If it was a non-fiction book, you may have visited the author's website and social media to see what other books, programs, or services they had to offer, and/or left a review on Amazon.

Take a moment to consider what action you'd like your reader to take once they've completed your impactful book. Do you have a program that would allow them to delve deeper into the concepts you introduced in your book? Perhaps you offer private sessions or group coaching and you'd like to invite them to schedule a discovery call. You could simply list out your products and services, or lead them to your website or Facebook group. Or, you might ask them to head to Amazon and leave an honest review if you don't currently have any other offers.

Whatever your goal, think of the back of your book as prime real estate and your final opportunity to invite your reader into your community or to become your client. End with a call to action and let them know how to continue the journey with you or how to get more help. Once you get to the back of this book, pay attention to how I have the ending structured. Because of course, I'd love to have YOU become my client, or at least a part of my valued community.

CHAPTER 4

The Many Phases
of a Manuscript

This chapter isn't meant to scare you, but rather to help you understand how your manuscript will change and evolve before it's ready for publication. It's also meant to remind you not to be too hard on yourself while writing that first draft, because the truth is, the draft you have on your completion date is only the first of many.

Remember, your book is a representation of you and your brand. You can't skimp on professional editing and proofreading, so don't rush this process just to get your book published quicker or to save on expenses. This is one expense you cannot afford to miss. Nothing will cause you to lose credibility faster than publishing a book littered with typos and grammatical errors, and you only get one chance to make a first impression on new readers.

Preparing Your Manuscript for Professional Editing

Once you complete your first draft, I recommend setting it aside for a few days, maybe even a week or two, and then doing something special to reward yourself for all your hard work. This is an amazing accomplishment, after all! Then, when it's time to return to your manuscript and create the second draft that you'll submit for editing, you'll go through it with fresh eyes and perform a much more efficient self-edit. Indeed, you may be amazed how that short break has allowed you to see it in a new light.

Success Tip: Read your manuscript aloud or have Microsoft Word read it to you through their Read Aloud feature, or you can also use naturalreaders.com. Our eyes naturally autocorrect small mistakes while viewing our own writing, so reading it aloud or having it read to you will help to "hear" run-on sentences, oddly-structured sentences, and missing or incorrect words, such as "form" when you meant "from." These are all things that sometimes the eyes won't catch.

NOTE: If you plan to enlist beta readers to offer feedback on your manuscript, I recommend doing so *before* your book goes to editing because you'll likely make changes to your manuscript based on their feedback. Your beta reader should be someone who is an ideal reader/client who will read your manuscript and then offer you thoughts on what you may have left out, things that did not make sense to them, or things you could omit.

Be very clear when working with beta readers exactly what you're looking for, and be sure to let them know they are receiving an unedited manuscript and that you're not looking for them to point out typos or grammatical errors, but rather to offer feedback on the manuscript as a whole to ensure it includes everything they would be looking for as your ideal reader.

I personally do not work with beta readers and elect only to work with professional book editors because there is always a risk of having your work stolen when sending out your manuscript prior to publication. Make sure you trust your beta readers if you decide to go that route, and also that they are your ideal audience for your book; otherwise their feedback may not be relevant or valuable to your topic or genre.

Finding a Professional Editor

If you're working with a self-publishing company that offers all-inclusive packages, they'll likely have editors on their team and include this in your package. However, if you're going this journey alone, here are a few places you can look for an editor to work with:

- Word-of-mouth – Ask your author friends if they have a recommendation
- Freelance sites such as Upwork.com or Freelancer.com
- Reedsy
- LinkedIn
- Independent editing and ghostwriting companies

Wherever you find your editor, the important thing is that they are a professional, not your aunt who is a schoolteacher or your best friend who's also an author. Why? Because there is so much more that goes into editing a book than looking for grammar and punctuation. A professional book editor will have a keen understanding of the structure and components of an impactful book that I have been discussing. They will also be able to step into the shoes of your ideal reader and either point out to you, or correct themselves, areas that can be omitted or fleshed out. They will also alert you to potential legal issues such as quoting copyrighted song lyrics without permission and using the real names of persons who have not consented and can sue you for libel. Now, this cannot be construed as legal advice unless your editor also happens to be a licensed attorney, however, being aware of red flags gives you the opportunity to make changes or consult a lawyer. Sometimes, but not always, it's helpful if your editor has previous experience with or knowledge of your particular genre or subject matter, as they will know when something you've written is inaccurate or could be explained further. Perhaps most importantly, a professional editor will always strive to preserve your unique voice.

Success Tip: Ask for a sample edit before you hire an editor. Most editors will offer a free sample edit of at least one chapter. It's important that you jive well with the editor you select, and getting a sample edit allows you to get a feel for their editing style, how deep they dig, how they deliver feedback, and overall how good they are at their job.

Revision Phase

Once you select an editor and they complete your initial edit, there will likely be some comments in the sidebar for you to address. Remember, a good editor will not only perform a line edit, but will look for places where you could strengthen your work, expand upon a concept you've introduced, or rephrase things that don't make sense.

Now it's time for you to perform your revision and craft your next draft. At this point you'll want to read each of the editor's comments and add or adjust things per their recommendation, and then read the manuscript again as a whole to ensure you're happy with all the changes. Sometimes an editor will change a word that just doesn't resonate with you, so you'll want to make additional tweaks.

Just as I suggested earlier that you read your manuscript aloud or have it read to you, I recommend it again after you've completed your revisions and before you submit it for copy/line editing.

Copy Editing

Once you have prepared your revised draft, I recommend having the same editor perform a second pass on your manuscript so they can see how you've addressed their recommendations. They'll also need to go through your manuscript again as a whole, this time performing more of a line edit to ensure it's polished and ready for interior formatting and design.

Interior Formatting

If you've followed the steps above, at this point you should be ready to have your book laid out for print by a professional book formatter. This is another expense you won't want to skimp on because, again, your book is a representation of you and your business. Bad formatting will make the book look DIY, and the goal of successful self-publishing is that your book should never appear self-published. So enlist the help of professionals to help you produce the most high-quality book possible with the proper margins, gutters, headers, footers, etc.

Success Tip: A good formatter will pull some of the design elements and fonts from your cover design into the interior design, so in my business we like to finalize the front cover before we begin interior design for our clients.

Once the book is laid out for print, you'll receive a PDF proof for review. You'll want to go through it carefully, and again, I recommend you read it aloud. You'll view your book differently once you see it laid out for print so you may request some additional tweaks at this point. You should also check for any formatting errors that may have occurred during the design process.

When selecting a formatter, be sure to ask how many rounds of revisions they include. For instance, at Transcendent Publishing, we include a total of three interior proofs with our packages.

Adding Endorsements

If you are sending your book out to credible professionals to ask for an endorsement, it's a good idea to wait until you have the formatted interior proof. You'll want your book to look as polished and professional as possible before you start asking others to review it and write an endorsement. For my clients, I usually recommend they send the formatted interior PDF proof only after it's gone through at least one round of proofing so it's clean. Once you've gathered your endorsements, your formatter can create a Praise page at the front of your book to feature them, or you can select your best ones to feature on the back cover.

Endorsements are optional, but sometimes an author will feel their book has more credibility if a well-known or credible professional endorses it. If you decide to ask someone to write an endorsement for you, don't just send them your book in the initial email, assuming they are going to say yes. You'll want to query them first and only send your book over after they've agreed.

Keep in mind, people we ask for endorsements are typically busy, so you'll want to allow them ample time but with a concrete deadline of when you'll need it back. Sometimes they won't have time to read your book at all, and will instead ask for a synopsis and opening chapter, or they will ask you to send over three possible endorsements written by you that they can choose from and add their name to, so don't be surprised if you receive that request.

Proofreading the Print-Ready PDF

Before you upload your book files to the printer, it's a good idea to have a proofreader read through the final PDF print-ready proof to ensure it's free of errors or last-minute typos that may have slipped through. It's also a good idea for you to give it one final read-through as well.

If there are any last-minute errors, have your formatter make the changes to the master file and create a revised PDF.

A note on typos: Even when a book is professionally edited and proofread, and you've combed through it several times yourself, it's not uncommon for a typo to slip through. If one is found post-publication, try not to beat yourself up too much about it. Have your formatter fix the typo and upload a revised file. That's the nice thing about print-on-demand, after all. Remember to correct it in both the paperback and e-book.

CHAPTER 5

Two Things You Must Never Forget to Add if You're Publishing a Book for Your Business

There are two key sections you should include in your book, especially if you want to turn your readers into clients, students, members, fans, etc.

1. Bonus gift
2. Call to action

Bonus Gift

We'll start with your bonus, which is a free gift you'll offer your readers in exchange for their contact information. This is how you'll deliver additional value to your readers while also adding more names to your mailing list. Unfortunately, Amazon and the other online retailers do not give authors contact information for their readers, so it's up to us to capture that for ourselves. Your mailing list is gold and the key to long-term success as an author, so don't skip this step.

How do we do it? By giving away something of value that complements or supplements our book's topic. This can be something as simple as a PDF checklist, cheatsheet, workbook, guide, or bonus chapter. If you want to get more in-depth, you may offer a mini video series, masterclass, or MP3 download. The sky's the limit when coming up with your bonus, and I've worked with authors who have used everything from a free coloring page to a guided meditation.

In my experience, a simple checklist or cheatsheet seems to convert well because readers like downloadable tools that will help them implement what you are teaching inside your book. Plus, it's easy to make a checklist or cheatsheet in Microsoft Word and convert it to a PDF. If you want a bit more design options, Canva has many free templates you can use, and then you simply convert the file to a PDF and download it. (You'll notice I've offered a Self-Publishing Success Checklist as the free bonus gift that accompanies this book. I created that in Canva with one of their free templates.)

Next, I created a landing page for my bonus gift, where I collect my readers' contact information. Once a reader opts in and joins my list, they receive a welcome message that delivers the PDF; they will also land on a thank you/confirmation page where they can download it as well, in case my email bounces or gets filtered as spam.

Now that they are on my list, it's my job to nurture my subscribers and keep them "warm." This is why I follow the welcome message with an auto-responder series of emails that are set to automatically deliver every few days for a week or so. This way, my new subscriber can get used to hearing from me and begin to know and trust me. These consist of a welcome email, followed by a backstory email, another that offers even more value, an email that lets them know how we can work together, and so on. Now, each time I launch a new book or program, I have a warm list of subscribers who are already interested in my content.

It's much easier to get book sales and reviews when you have a mailing list of people who are interested in you and what you have to offer, so it's imperative that you begin building your list right away. While you're writing your book, you can offer a free gift on your website, blog, and social media profiles to begin building your list now so you have an audience to announce your book to once it's ready.

If you'd like to see how this is done, you can check out my opt-in funnel here: www.shandatrofe.com/checklist. My feelings won't be hurt if you subscribe just to see my process and then unsubscribe, but, of course, I'd love it if you'd become a longtime subscriber. I try to send more value emails than sales emails (a good rule of thumb to follow), and I promise not to spam you. You'll receive writing and self-publishing tips, free resources, and then occasionally I'll let you know when I have a new program launching or space for a one-on-one client opens.

Call to Action

Now, let's talk about your call to action. This is where the real money is made by authors, through backend sales.

As mentioned earlier, you have probably read a book you loved so much you didn't want it to end. Before you even reached the last page, you found yourself wondering what else the author had published so you could continue consuming their content, and possibly Googled them to find their website, sought them out on LinkedIn or Facebook, found a way to join their mailing list, etc. so you could further delve into what they introduced inside the book.

Don't make this hard on your readers. They should never have to go searching to find a way to work with you or consume your other content. Utilize the back of your book as a place to offer your readers a way to continue the journey with you.

If you're like me, when reading a book you enjoy, you also want to know everything about the author. That's why I like to end each book with an About the Author page along with my contact information, including my business email address, website, and social media profiles. It's up to you how much information you'd like to share, but think of your book like a business card, because it's essentially the next best thing! If you'd put it on your business card, why not put it inside a book written for your business? The only thing I don't include is a phone number, for obvious reasons, although I have seen authors include a business number as well.

While you're at it, don't forget to add your bio. I can't tell you the number of authors I've worked with who don't want to put their bios inside their book because they've put it on the back cover. The problem with that is people who find your book online usually download the e-book, so they never even see the back cover. That's why I advise my clients to put their full bio and contact information inside the book on the About the Author page, and put their short bio and headshot on the back cover, along with a book blurb and maybe an endorsement or two. We'll get into those details later, but for now, make sure you tell your readers about you, and more importantly, how they can find and connect with you once they are finished reading your valuable content.

Following the closing of the book, or after the About the Author and contact information, is where I like to place the call to action. In this book, my call-to-action page is titled, "How to Get More Help." The call to action lets your reader know about your best offer. If you worry that your offer may change over time, no problem. That's the beauty of self-publishing. You can always upload a revised file if your offer changes or your program goes away, but as a general rule of thumb, make your call to action something that you plan on having around for a while such as another one of your book(s), a complimentary strategy session, online course, membership program—you get the gist.

Are you a coach who offers a free discovery call? Let your readers know and add a link to your scheduler. Do you have an online course that accompanies the book? Share a discount code to save on enrollment as a thank you for being a valued reader. Have another book you'd like them to read? Share the cover, blurb and a link to Amazon or your website, or list all of your products and services on a page with a link of where to learn more.

Again, the call-to-action page is your place to convert your readers to clients or lifelong fans, so don't waste this space. If they've made it to the back of your book, chances are they'd like to continue on with you, so make it as easy as possible to find you and form a connection.

CHAPTER 6

The DOs and DON'Ts
of Self-Publishing Success

Before I walk you through the steps of successful self-publishing, I want to begin by shedding light on some of the common mistakes I've witnessed from indie authors who set out to go it alone and learn as they go.

Self-Publishing Mistakes to Avoid

In my business, I've been working closely with self-published authors since 2012. Over the years, I've witnessed many mistakes made by first-time authors, not to mention the number of authors who come to me for help publishing a second edition of their book because the first fell flat.

So, what causes a book to fail?

Either the author didn't know *how* to market their book, so it never got the proper sales, ranking, or traction to reach its potential, or they were in a hurry to get the book out and rushed through the production process, skimping on the small details that make up a high-quality book. I don't want this to happen to you, so in this chapter I'm going to share what *not* to do so that you self-publish your book right the *first* time and avoid costly mistakes.

First, I want to clear up a common publishing misconception. Some used to believe that self-publishing was only for those who couldn't get picked up by a traditional publisher. They thought traditional publishing was the only respectable route and considered self-publishing second best.

Well, luckily for you, those days are long behind us!

Today, self-publishing is the popular choice, and indie authors are on the rise as more and more authors discover they can retain the majority of their royalties and get their books published faster while maintaining creative control over the entire process, from idea to publication.

For these reasons, even authors who were traditionally published in the past are switching over to self-publishing, especially since the majority of book marketing efforts are now made by the author, no matter which publishing path they choose.

Indeed, the days of traditional publishers funding book promotions for their authors are long gone—the exception being those in their top 3% of earners. The other authors on their rosters can expect some assistance with regard to marketing efforts, but the lion's share of the work (including growing their platforms) will fall on them.

Considering all these factors, it's no wonder more and more authors are choosing self-publishing without even bothering to seek an agent and/or traditional publisher, or that those who were previously traditionally published are jumping ship over to the indie author world. And, there's absolutely nothing wrong with that ... when it's done *correctly*.

The key is to self-publish a high-quality book that doesn't *appear* self-published, as this will bring you credibility as an indie author. The way you do that is to invest both time and money to create a book you can be proud of and are excited to promote. Many indie authors, especially first-time authors, will rush through the process in an attempt to get their book done as quickly as possible or to save a few dollars. Unfortunately, these decisions can be detrimental to the future success of the book, so taking time to do it right from the start will ultimately save you time and money in the long run.

In the pages ahead, I've compiled a list of the top six mistakes I see indie authors make when self-publishing. Avoid these mistakes from the start, and you'll craft a high-quality book that allows you to shine, and with a lot less mess to clean up down the road.

1. Losing steam after the initial launch.

I've seen this happen time and time again. An author will set out to publish and launch their book and the next thing you know it falls flat ... maybe not at first, but eventually.

Why? Well, birthing a book can be a long, exhausting process. First, you must write the book, and that typically takes several drafts and revisions before the production process begins. Then formatting and design starts, and so begins even more revisions. Setting up a book launch, getting reviews, announcing publication to the world—it can all be rather tiring.

At first, the author seems all-in, blasting their list and social media with book announcements, followed by a series of interviews and media appearances to let the world know their book is published...

Fast forward three to six months ... *crickets.*

What happened? Chances are the author gave their all to the writing, publishing and launch of the book; it's a big job, after all. So, after the initial buzz wears off, the author takes a much-needed break from the project.

The problem is, right after the initial launch is when book marketing is crucial. Some say that's when the *real* work begins as an author, so it is NOT the time to drop the ball! If you're going to put the time and effort into writing a book, and so much energy into the creation of the project, don't stop short of the victory.

Commit to doing a minimum of one thing each day to market your book upon publication, such as reaching out to a podcast host for an interview or pitching a guest blog article idea to a popular blogger in your niche. Don't worry, not every day has to be a time-consuming effort. It can be something as simple as scheduling a bargain book promotion on your e-book, or offering a value post on social media related to your topic or area of expertise.

The point is, don't give your book a year of your life just to let it fall flat after the high of the initial launch wears off. There are over 57 million books on Amazon[11], so it's not enough just to publish and think readers will find it. We must always be promoting and driving traffic to the book, so keep the pace and the momentum going for the project long *after* publication.

2. Failing to plan a strategic launch.

The only thing worse than letting your book launch fall flat is failing to launch in the first place.

Why would anyone do that? Well, it happens more often than you might think, and for a number of reasons.

First, the author might not know *how* to market their book, so they think they can simply upload it to Amazon, press that magical "publish" button, and watch the sales roll in. Sadly, that's not the case. The question is, how do you expect your book to stand out in a crowd without a solid marketing campaign in place?

Set yourself up for success by thoroughly planning out the timeline of your launch *before* publication day. Research and brainstorm ways to drive traffic to your book and, most importantly, begin building your author platform *long* before publication so you have an engaged audience to market your book to once that day arrives.

---

[11] https://www.scrapehero.com/how-many-products-does-amazon-sell-march-2021/

3. DIY covers.

Do-it-yourself covers … just *don't* do it. Unfortunately, people *do* judge books by their covers, so unless you are a trained graphic designer, do not, I repeat, DO NOT attempt to create your own book cover.

This is an amateur move, and it's obvious to the trained eye. Not to mention, it will likely cost you more time and money in the long run. Let me explain…

I can't tell you how many authors I've seen try to design their own cover, usually one they've created with Canva or PicMonkey. That's fine because it offers the professional designers you hand it off to a feel for your vision; however, creating a front cover using free online software does not equate to a print-ready cover.

First of all, the full print-ready cover is a PDF file of the front, back and spine that wraps the book and gets uploaded to the printer as one file. It is sized based on the final page count of the interior file, so the dimensions depend on it. Get it wrong and your cover will be rejected.

If you create your own cover, you'll need to not only know about design elements such as color and font pairings and where to aesthetically place text and graphics, but where to place the barcode, the width of the spine, the bleed, etc.

You should not only outsource cover design because a high-quality cover will help sell your book, but also because it will save you valuable time and money in the long run by preventing your file from being rejected by the printer.

In today's competitive market, cover design can make or break your book. There are many affordable designers who do high-quality work, so you don't have to spend a fortune, but this is one expense you don't want to skip. You can always maintain creative control over the design and show a mockup of your vision, but I find the best covers are created when we allow our cover artist to do what he or she does best.

Success Tip: The only thing worse than not giving your designer any direction is giving him or her too much guidance. Offer your designer a feel for your vision and then allow them the freedom to use their creativity and expertise.

4. Passing on professional editing.

After staring at our own writing for so long, rereading our manuscript over and over, making tweaks and revisions, our eyes grow used to the words on the paper/screen, and we naturally begin to skip over errors. We simply cannot edit our own writing, at least not to the level it needs to be for a professional book.

As mentioned earlier, I do highly recommend crafting several revised drafts before passing your manuscript on to a professional editor, but if you think you can edit your own manuscript to save funds, or use software such as Grammarly in place of a professional book editor, you are setting yourself up for failure (not to mention embarrassment).

Skipping this detail may be detrimental to the success of your book, and therefore rob your business of an excellent opportunity for growth. Find a professional editor, invest the time and the money, and the quality of your book will benefit, I promise you that.

5. Using a free ISBN

Some print-on-demand publishing platforms will supply a free ISBN unless you supply your own. Yes, using a free ISBN will save you between $99-$125, but there is a significant downside, namely:

1. That platform now owns your ISBN, therefore, you can't publish your book elsewhere without creating a new edition.
2. It tells the world your book is self-published.

When you use a free ISBN, the publishing imprint on your book's Amazon page is listed as *Independently Published*. If you want to tell the world your book is self-published, then go ahead and take this route.

However, if you want to self-publish a high-quality book that doesn't *appear* self-published, then you'll want to add your own publishing imprint, and to do this, we must own our ISBN, which you can purchase from Bowker here in the US.

Create a professional publishing imprint to assign to your ISBN, and when you self-publish your book, your chosen publishing imprint will be listed as the publisher instead of *Independently Published*.

Having a custom imprint will kick your book's quality up a notch, so this is another investment well worth the cost when self-publishing. Plus, if you plan to publish more books, this will come in handy down the road.

6. Skimping on the small details to save time and money.

The other reason an author may fail to set up a proper book launch and marketing campaign is because they rushed through the production process, skipping over important details in an attempt to save money.

What they are left with is a book they're not proud of and perhaps even embarrassed to announce to the world. That's why it's so important to take your time and invest in the components that make up a high-quality book such as a professional cover design, editing and proofreading, and quality interior formatting and design.

Publishing a book is an investment in your future, and your book is an extension of *you*. If you can't afford to do it right the first time, you'll likely end up releasing a revised edition down the road. Better to save up and hold off until you can afford to invest in the small details that make your self-published book look as professional as possible.

Remember, the goal is to create a book as professionally as possible, so as not to lose credibility in today's competitive market.

The 9 Key Components of a Bestselling Book

Now that you've learned what not to do and common mistakes to avoid, let's review the key components that make up a bestselling book.

1. **High-end cover design.** As mentioned, readers *will* judge your book by its cover, so make sure to set yourself up for success. A high-quality design will set your book apart

from the competition so that it stands out in your genre, grabs the attention of your ideal reader, and is designed to convert to sales.

2. **An enticing book blurb.** While the cover attracts your ideal reader, your book description is what prompts them to hit that "Buy Now" button. Make sure it tells enough to draw your reader in, and highlights the key benefits. Consider ending your blurb with a call to action prompting your reader to buy.

3. **Interior formatting.** Quality interior formatting will pull elements from your cover and carry them into the interior design. Seek out a custom interior design exclusive to your book to give it a professional look that WOWs your readers.

4. **An imprint-assigned ISBN.** Never use a free ISBN unless you want your book to be married to the print-on-demand platform providing it. Plus, an ISBN should be assigned to a publishing imprint so that it does not say "Independently Published" in your book's product listing with online retailers.

5. **Professional editing.** Nothing will cause an author to lose credibility faster than publishing a book without professional editing. Your book needs to be polished, and that takes a few sets of eyes other than your own.

6. **SEO-optimized metadata.** Your title, subtitle, book description, and keyword tags play an active role in your book showing up in searches via online retailers. For long-term sales, your metadata needs to be optimized for SEO (Search Engine Optimization) so your book does not get lost in the sea of competition!

7. **Strategic book launch.** You only get one chance to launch your book to the world! This is when you'll gain reviews, earn your bestseller badge, and ignite Amazon's powerful algorithm. A strategic launch will set you up for long-term success as an author.

8. **Solid marketing plan.** You'll need an ongoing marketing plan for long-term success as an author. Your job isn't finished once your book is published and launched. Keeping your book in front of your target audience and ideal readers should become an everyday goal and ongoing mission.

9. **Invaluable content.** This goes without saying, but none of what I've shared above will help unless you've written a great book that delivers on its promise. Follow the I.M.P.A.C.T. acronym I shared in the Introduction to ensure you've structured your book in a way that will engage your ideal readers and leave them with actionable, measurable steps to deliver on your promise.

In the following chapters, I'm going to break down these must-have components in greater detail.

CHAPTER 7

Setting Up Your Publishing Imprint and Business (Yes, self-publishing is a business!)

If you are delving into the world of self-publishing, then you'll want to treat your imprint as a business, especially if you plan to write and publish more books. One reason is that there are tax perks for your publishing business when it's set up properly. Since I'm not a tax professional or an attorney, I can't offer specifics on forming your business; plus, the logistics will vary by state. I can tell you, however, that you may want to set up either a sole proprietorship or an LLC. Whatever you decide, you should speak to a CPA or an attorney to find the best course of action for your situation.

If you already have a business, you could possibly create your publishing imprint under the umbrella of your main business by filing a fictitious name registration or DBA (Doing Business As). For example, my main business is Write from the Heart LLC, and my publishing imprints are DBAs under that LLC.

At this point you may be wondering, *What is a publishing imprint?* That's the name that will be listed under the publishing information when you publish a book. You'll add your imprint name in Bowker, where you'll purchase your ISBN, and you'll assign your ISBN to that imprint. When it comes time to publish your book, you'll list your imprint name when adding the book's metadata in IngramSpark and/or KDP, or whichever distributor you choose. And when you set up your publishing accounts with those distributors, your royalties can be paid to your business and tax ID number instead of your name and social security number, which means you'll be able to take advantage of certain business tax write-offs for that income. Plus, if you decide to create an LLC for your publishing business your personal assets will have a certain level of protection as well.

You may be thinking, "But Shanda, my best friend's cousin published a book on Amazon and she didn't set up a company. She just uploaded it to KDP and published." Yes, I know it's possible, but just because it's possible doesn't mean you should do it. Or maybe you should, because only you can decide what's best for you and your book. But I'm here to teach you how to publish a book that sets you up for long-term success, so unless you are working with a publishing company that is supplying an ISBN that's connected to their imprint, you will need to set up your own.

Remember, the key to successful self-publishing is to create a book that doesn't appear self-published. The words "Independently Published"—which is what online retailers will add by default if you use one of their free ISBNs—is a dead giveaway.

Instead, you want your prospects to go to the book's product page on Amazon and other online retailers and see the name of your custom imprint.

Choosing an Imprint Name

You'll want to conduct a Google search to ensure your imprint name is not already in use, and it's a good idea to do a trademark search as well (you do this for free at uspto.gov). I'm not saying you need to trademark your imprint name but, like I said, make sure no one else is already using it.

Also, consider adding a suffix onto the end of the imprint to offer it another level of professionalism. For example:

- Books
- Press
- Publishing
- Ink

Some authors simply use their name (i.e. Jane Doe) or the name of their LLC, and that's okay, but it's also a giveaway that the book is self-published. If your book takes off, you'll thank me later for having a strategic imprint listed. Also, if you plan on trying to hit a major bestseller list such as *USA Today* or *The Wall Street Journal*, you have a better chance of being chosen if you have a professional publishing imprint representing your book. This is why you won't see Write from the Heart LLC listed on any of my books, even though that's the main LLC for my business. You'll see one of my imprints.

To recap, here are your steps for setting up your publishing company and imprint:

1. Talk to a tax professional or attorney in your state to decide how to set up your publishing business (usually an LLC or Sole Proprietorship). Or, if you already have a business, you might be able to add it under that umbrella.

2. Decide on an imprint name.

3. Do a Google search and Trademark search to ensure your imprint name is not already in use.

4. Consider adding a suffix to offer a professional feel such as Books, Publishing, Press or Ink.

5. When you create your account with Bowker, add your company info and your imprint, then assign your ISBN to that imprint (this is one of the steps when you add your book title).

6. Create a business checking account and keep your publishing expenses and income separate from your personal expenditures.

7. Create your publishing accounts with IngramSpark and KDP where you'll likely distribute your book (and anywhere else you are distributing it), and add your company name, tax ID number, and business checking account so you can be paid royalties via direct deposit.

8. Upload your book and add your imprint name when you add the book's metadata for each title you are publishing.

This is not required and there are certainly many indie authors who instead either leave the publishing imprint blank, use their name or current business name, or use a free ISBN assigned by their distributor. But, again, if you want your book to look as professionally published as possible, then I highly recommend creating a unique imprint.

CHAPTER 8

Preparing to Publish

Now that you've written a high-quality book, and have everything needed to make it a bestseller, it's time to publish!

Before you choose a publishing platform and upload your files, there is some prep work you'll want to do first to set yourself up for success.

Conducting Market Research

One of the first steps—and this can be helpful before you even begin writing—is to conduct market research for your book. I've found that Amazon is the best place to do this, although you could certainly take the time to conduct this same research on other book seller platforms as well. However, Amazon holds the largest market share for online book sales, so if you only have time to do this in one place, Amazon is a great choice and the one I personally use for all of my market research.

Start a spreadsheet to record your findings, and spend an hour or so conducting market research on your topic, genre, and competition. This will not only set your book up for success, but it can save you from making unnecessary mistakes by finding what's trending, what's working and what isn't working in your genre, and for other authors in your realm.

During your market research session, you'll peruse Amazon by first typing your main topic or keyword into the Amazon search bar. What keywords and keyword phrases does Amazon auto-populate from the dropdown menu? Take note of those phrases, because at the time of your search those are the most searched phrases on Amazon in relation to that keyword. Write them down so you can later add them to your title, subtitle, book description or hidden keyword tags when it comes time to publish.

For example, for this book, I might type "self-publishing" into the search bar. Let's see what Amazon populates:

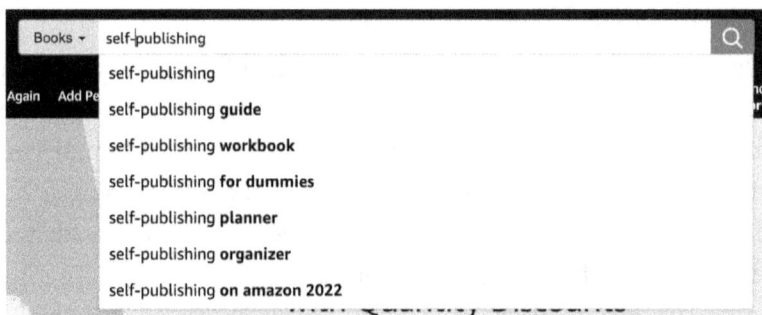

I might repeat this process several times with different keywords relevant to my book, such as:

- Authorship
- Write a book
- Book-writing
- How to self-publish
- Authorpreneur

And so on.

Next, you'll want to see which books each of your main keywords populates. This is a great way to scope out the competition and see other books in your genre. I like to review the first ten to twenty books that populate for each main keyword or keyword phrase most relevant to my book. For this book, that would be "self-publishing," "write a book," and "authorship."

While reviewing these books, you'll want to take note of a few things:

- What do the covers look like? Do they have a certain feel?
- Are there design patterns and trends in your genre?
- What keywords/keyword phrases have your competitors chosen to use in their titles and subtitles that prompted their books to appear in this search?
- What does their book description say about their books and what's inside? How does the length vary from other book descriptions, and do you prefer reading longer or shorter ones? Do they have bold taglines at the top, and bullet points to highlight key benefits for the reader?

- What's the page count? (Hint: to get an accurate count you'll want to switch from Kindle to the paperback version, then scroll down the product page to the Product Details section.)

- What retail price have your competitors chosen for each format of their book? Keep in mind, you'll want to take page count into consideration when looking for comparable books.

Success Tip: Click on the "Look Inside" feature and review the table of contents. You would never want to copy everything someone else is putting in their book and the order in which they are delivering it, but this is a great way for you to ensure you haven't forgotten anything relevant to your topic.

For example, in reviewing the table of contents of other books in my genre, I kept seeing chapters or subchapters related to pricing. I realized I hadn't planned to cover how to price your book in my original outline. Pricing is certainly something I teach in my courses and to my clients, yet I had completely forgotten to include it in my outline for this book—a huge oversight on my part! So you see, doing this market research reminded me not to forget this important piece of info, which may have earned me a poor review. Which leads me to the next step…

Read the negative reviews on the bestselling books in your genre. This is one of the most valuable steps to this process. While some readers (who, mind you, will never understand what goes into writing and publishing a book), will leave bad reviews for no good reason, you will sometimes run across a review that lets you know what the author was missing, from a reader's perspective. And not just any reader—a reader from your target audience! Your ideal reader. Usually you'll find this info within the four- or three-star reviews or lower. If you read more than once that readers felt something was missing, and they are usually very specific, you may want to consider adding that to your book.

In reading my competitors' reviews during my market research for this book, I discovered a theme: a lack of information on marketing. I kept seeing, over and over again, bad reviews in my genre because the author did not explain ways to promote and market a book post-publication. That's why you'll find *23 Ways to Market Your Book Post-Publication* in a coming chapter.

While it's important to read the negative reviews, it can be just as telling to read the favorable five-star reviews. What did readers love about the book? For example, if you are writing a book on the keto diet and found that the five-star reviews included glowing praise for the inclusion of a grocery shopping guide, then you may want to consider including a shopping guide in your own book.

Again, you are not copying here, you're only using your market research session to discover what's trending in your genre, what's working and what isn't for your competition, and what readers loved and didn't like about other books on your topic. Spending an hour or so doing this will set you up for success and help you avoid mistakes such as choosing the wrong cover design, price point, missing out on relevant keywords, and important topics to include inside your book.

If you don't have time to conduct market research, you can utilize a tool such as Publisher Rocket for this process. It allows you to scope out the competition, and also offers insights on monthly income for other books in your genre. Kindle Spy is another valuable tool to make your market research easier, but these are paid tools. If you can spare an extra hour you can do it for free by following the steps mentioned above.

Selecting a Title and Subtitle that Sells

Once you've conducted your market research, you should have a list of keywords and keyword phrases that people are searching for on Amazon in relation to your topic. You're going to use these keywords and phrases in your book's metadata and here's why...

Amazon is the world's largest search engine for e-commerce[12]. If you want your book to appear in more searches, then it's imperative that you set up your book's product listing optimized for SEO. The way we do that is to put valuable keywords and phrases where we can, in this order of hierarchy:

- Title
- Subtitle
- Book Description
- Hidden Keyword Tags

The categories you select for your book are extremely important as well, and often they will contain your keywords, but we will discuss categories in detail a bit later in this chapter. For now, let's focus on your title and subtitle.

---

[12] https://moz.com/blog/amazon-vs-google

I like to think of titles and subtitles like this...

- Titles grab attention.
- Subtitles call out to your target audience and let them know what the book is about and their benefit for reading it.

While it's most helpful when we can put our main keyword in the title, sometimes that's just not an option. In fact, some of the best titles don't say much about the book at all. They are intriguing and attention-grabbing but they don't have a keyword, and that's okay, as long as they have a strong subtitle that does include those keywords and explains what the book is about.

Here are a few examples of catchy titles of bestselling books (without keywords):

Eat That Frog by Brian Tracy

Girl, Wash Your Face by Rachel Hollis

The E-Myth by Michael Gerber

As you'll notice, those all have intriguing titles that grab your attention, but then rely on the subtitle to tell you what the book is actually about:

*Eat That Frog: **21 Great Ways to Stop Procrastinating and Get More Done in Less Time***

*Girl, Wash Your Face: **Stop Believing the Lies About Who You Are So You Can Become Who You Were Meant to Be***

The E-Myth: **Why Most Businesses Don't Work and What to Do About It**

That said, if you are able to create a title with keywords your book will likely show up in more searches. Ultimately, only you can decide whether you want to go with a catchy title to grab attention, or one that includes your main keyword.

Take the title of this book, for example. I placed my main keyword, "self-publishing," right in the title: *Self-Publishing Success.* So if someone types self-publishing into the Amazon search bar, my book will likely show up in that search (with a few other variables to consider such as search volume, sales ranking, and such).

However, I could have gone with an intriguing title that may have grabbed attention, but it wouldn't have appeared in as many searches for books on self-publishing. In that case, I would have made sure to utilize the keyword "self-publishing" in the subtitle.

Even if your title does include your main keyword, you can still include keywords in your subtitle as well. For example, though I used my main keyword—"self-publishing"—in my title, I also worked in other strong keyword phrases—"write a book"; "how to write a book"; "non-fiction book" and "publish"—into the subtitle. In doing this, I made sure it called out to my target audience: aspiring authors looking to write a book and self-publish.

Self-Publishing Success: **How to Write a Non-Fiction Book** That Makes an Impact and **Publish** it Like a Pro.

Since I have three of my strongest keywords/keyword phrases in my title and subtitle (I've put them in bold for you), now my book will show up in plenty of searches, depending on what my ideal reader types into the Amazon search bar. This is a great way to keep your book in front of your target audience organically. Don't get me wrong, you'll still need to ignite Amazon's algorithm through a strategic book launch and continue to market your book, but this will help with organic sales that happen while you sleep, and what's better than that?

Tips for creating a title and subtitle that sells:

- Choose a title that's either catchy or includes your main keyword. I prefer the latter.

- The best titles are short (1 to 3 words). Save the details for the subtitle.

- Your subtitle should call out to your ideal reader, and they should be able to read the subtitle and know exactly what your book is about and what benefit they will receive by reading it. This is especially important if you don't put your main keyword in your title.

- Add a keyword/phrase or two, but be mindful not to "keyword stuff" as that's frowned upon by Amazon.

- Do not use the same keyword twice, as it's against Amazon's terms of service. For instance, if I had *Self-Publishing Success: How to Write a Non-Fiction Book that Makes an Impact and Self-Publish it Like a Pro*, Amazon may have flagged my book and removed it from sale. I've seen it happen on day one of an author's launch, which caused a world of trouble and embarrassment for the author, so do not make that mistake.

Writing Your Book Blurb

As I said earlier, while the cover grabs a potential reader's attention, the book blurb is what prompts them to buy, so an enticing blurb is equally as important to your book's success. What's a blurb? It's the description that will appear on Amazon and other online retailers that tells what your book is about. Often the same words will be used on the back cover of your book as well, but the two don't have to match.

Recall my suggestion that during your market research you read the blurbs of the bestselling books in your genre. Hopefully you took note of the blurbs that stood out to you, and the ones that you actually took the time to read in full. I find that when a blurb is too long, a prospect won't always take the time to read it, so I like to aim for a blurb of three-hundred words or fewer.

This is the formula I like to follow when writing a blurb for a non-fiction book, especially one for business. I break it into four sections:

Section 1: Start with an enticing, bolded tagline. This is a statement of one to two sentences that makes a bold claim, in bold font, to call out to your ideal reader and grab their attention. Here are some examples of strong taglines from bestselling books:

1. *Atomic Habits* by James Clear. Book blurb tagline: ***Tiny Changes, Remarkable Results.***

2. *Rich as F*ck* by Amanda Frances. Book blurb tagline: **Ready for more money than you know what to do with?**

3. *The 80/20 Principle* by Richard Koch. Book Blurb tagline: **Be more effective with less effort by learning how to identify and leverage the 80/20 principle: that 80 percent of all our results in business and in life stem from a mere 20 percent of our efforts.**

Some are short and to the point, while others are a sentence or two. All, however, are designed to grab your reader's attention with a bold statement or question that entices them to continue reading.

Section 2: Enticing opening paragraph. After you've written a bold headline, skip a space and add the opening paragraph. This is where you'll want to put the most important information about the book because it's often all the prospect sees. Why? Because a book's product page on Amazon only shows the first paragraph or so before they offer a clickable "read more" link that opens the rest of the description.

Not everyone clicks the "read more" link, so you'll need to put your most enticing yet relevant information about your book in that first paragraph.

Section 3: Bullet Points that feature the book's benefits. Even those who click the read more link won't always read the entire book description; however, they are more likely to skim through bullet points since they usually highlight the benefits and main takeaways of the book. So ask yourself: What are five main takeaways from my book? Do they benefit my reader in some way? How can I word my bullet points so they're enticing and packed with value? Here's a tip: If you know your prospects' pain points, your bullet points should be the answer to their problem.

Section 4: A closing paragraph that prompts them to buy. Finally, end your blurb with a closing paragraph that leaves your prospect inspired to take action. Often this will include a call to action to buy now.

As an example, head to Amazon and read the blurb for this book, and while you're there, check out blurbs by some of the masters such as Bryan Cohen, who also offers a blurb-writing service through his company Best Page Forward, for those who don't want to go this alone. At the very least, I highly recommend his book, *How to Write a Sizzling Synopsis,* if you'd like more details about how to write a great blurb.

Selecting the Retail Price for Your Paperback and E-book

While I can give you an idea for how to price your book, there are always exceptions to the rule, and pricing trends tend to vary by genre, which is another reason I recommend Amazon market research before you settle on your pricing structure.

Let's start with the e-book. There really are so many variables when it comes to pricing your book in this format.

Remember, if you're publishing your e-book through KDP, Amazon will pay you 70% royalties on the retail price when your e-book is priced between $2.99 and $9.99. Above or below that price range, you'll receive 35%. If you are going wide with your e-book, meaning you are not offering Amazon exclusivity but are also selling it via other online e-book retailers such as iBooks, Kobo, Nook, etc., your royalties will typically range between 40 and 60% of the retail price, depending on where you're distributing it.

As mentioned in an earlier chapter, we'll often discount the e-book to $.99 during the launch to bestseller. We might also price the book below $2.99 when it's a first in series; this strategy is used to attract new readers in the hopes that they will continue to read each subsequent book in the series at a slightly higher price than the first. So you see, there are times when it makes sense to price the e-book at a low price point and take the lower royalty.

That said, in my experience testing my e-books and those of my clients, the sweet spot for self-published non-fiction e-books seems to be between $3.99 and $6.99, with my favorite price point being $4.99. If that feels low to you, then you could test the range of $6.99 to $9.99. Again, this will depend on length and genre, so it's important to do your market research, and even then you may decide you want the highest price point possible without pricing yourself out of the 70% royalty range and go with $9.99, which is more commonly seen with traditionally published books.

For this book's digital edition, I found in my market research that other authors with e-books of a similar length ranged from $3.99 to $6.99. It feels good to me to stay in that range since my goal is not necessarily to make a million dollars off the sale of this book (although that'd be nice!), but rather to get as many readers to find my book as possible (more readers mean more potential clients); plus, with a low price point, I have the opportunity to get a higher volume of sales. In other words, the focus of my strategy is not on royalties, but on the potential back-end sales if my readers decide they want to work with me or enroll in one of my programs in the future.

On the other hand, I have a client who specializes in coaching male entrepreneurs and CEOs. He's a high-level coach who charges in the high five figures to work with him. He has one flagship book for his business; it's full length coming in at just over 40,000 words. He packs insane value into his book, but his ultimate goal for writing it was to attract high-level clients who can afford to work with him, therefore, we've priced his e-book at $9.99. He knows this price point may deter some readers, but that's okay because in his mind those people probably can't afford to work with him anyway. So you see, the higher pricing is not only a way to show perceived value for his book but to weed out anyone who is not his ideal client, therefore, he's willing to lose some sales.

I have another client who sells his paperback through a "free + shipping" book funnel. The idea of that type of book funnel is that you give away a free copy of your paperback (usually on your website or a landing page), but only charge for shipping. Once the prospect enters their credit card information to pay for the shipping, they are redirected to an upsell page or two where the author makes additional paid offers such as an online course, membership program, a one-on-one session, or mastermind.

Authors usually charge between $7.95 and $9.95 for shipping through these types of book funnels in order to cover their own costs on printing and shipping of the books. In this case, my client did *not* want his e-book to sell via online retailers that would take away from his book funnel; therefore, he listed his e-book for $9.99 and his paperback for $19.99 on Amazon and other retailers.

There were two reasons for this strategy: 1) It lent more perceived value to his book to give it away for free through his funnel when it was listed at a high price point elsewhere; 2) It lessened the risk of losing potential sales through his funnel, which he certainly may have if he priced it lower on Amazon and readers opted for this "bargain."

So, first decide on your goal. Would you like to get as many readers as possible? If so, then a lower price point may be the way to go. If you don't mind losing out on some sales and want to prequalify prospective clients, then a higher price point may be for you. It's always going to be important to know your target audience, and know your genre before settling on a price point.

The nice thing about e-book pricing is that it can easily be changed, so you can always start low and gradually raise your price, testing each price range to find your sweet spot.

Now, let's talk about pricing your paperback. Before deciding on a retail price, it's important to estimate your cost of printing, since before your royalties are calculated the cost of printing will be deducted from the retail price, along with any additional distribution costs.

The first thing to ask yourself is whether you are printing your book with a color or black and white interior, because that will make a major difference in your printing cost (color printing is quite expensive). That said, sometimes an author will opt for color printing, for example, if they have photos that they want to feature in color inside the book. In this case, you'll want to price out your cost of printing with your print-on-demand printer ahead of time, as they will often set a minimum price point for you to list as the retail price based on your print cost.

However, since most authors print in black and white interior, we are going to assume, for the sake of this example, that you are doing the same. And in this example, I am going to use the trim size of 5.5 x 8.5 (a popular choice for a non-fiction book), and a page count of 200.

If you are using IngramSpark and KDP for paperback distribution, which, as mentioned, is what I recommend (more on this later), it will, at the time of this writing, cost you an average of $3 to $4 to print. The price varies between the two platforms, with IngramSpark typically being a bit higher than KDP; however, with IngramSpark you have the opportunity to offer your paperback to retailers at a desirable 55% wholesale discount, which is what most like to see.

Here's how your royalty would be calculated with IngramSpark if we were to select a retail price of $16.99, which is just a price I selected for this example and not necessarily what I recommend.

First you subtract the 55% wholesale discount that retailers will receive from IngramSpark, then subtract the cost of printing, and what's left is your royalty.

$16.99 - 55% = $9.35 - $4.00 (cost of printing) = $3.65 royalty per online sale

If you go with KDP, your royalty will be 60% (the fixed royalty rate KDP offers on paperbacks sold on Amazon marketplaces where KDP supports paperback distribution), less the cost of printing.

60% of $16.99 = $10.19 - $4.00 (cost of printing) = $6.19 royalty per Amazon sale

The printing costs depend on your book's page count and the Amazon marketplace from which your paperback was ordered. Sometimes your royalty will be slightly higher with KDP than with IngramSpark, which is why I recommend you distribute your paperback with both, but we will get into that in more detail in the next chapter.

So you see why it's important to figure out your printing costs before deciding on a retail price for your paperback. As with everything else, you'll also want to follow what you discovered during your market research so your pricing structure is in line with other books in your genre.

Success Tip: An easy way to estimate your book's cost to print is to use IngramSpark's book calculator or KDP's pricing resources. Keep in mind you'll need to know your book's trim size and estimated page count in print. It's important to note that your manuscript page count does not equate to your book's final page count once it's laid out for print, but you can estimate your printed page to have 250 to 300 words per page, depending on trim size, font size, spacing, number of graphics, etc. For example, you can estimate a 40,000-word manuscript, divided by 250, to be around 160 printed pages. But again, this will vary depending on the trim size and formatting.

Selecting a Trim Size for Your Book

The standard trim size is 6x9, however, I prefer a slightly smaller size of 5.5 x 8.5, which is quite popular among self-help, personal development, and business books. If you find your book falls short in word count and you'd like to give it additional length, you might consider one size down: 5.25 x 8.

If your book is more of a workbook, then 6 x 9 will usually work well, but you might go with a larger trim size such as 7 x 10 so your readers have more space to fill in answers to your journal prompts or exercise questions right inside the book. I've even had clients print their workbooks in size 8.5 x 11, but in my opinion 7 x 10 is a nice size for a workbook. I prefer journals at 6 x 9, and I usually reserve 5 x 8 for fiction.

You could always pull your favorite books off your bookshelf and measure the trim size to get a feel for the different sizes. Or, you could go to Amazon, search for those books, and find the dimensions listed under the product details section about midway down the page.

Having the Cover Designed

I know I've already touched on this, but it's worth repeating: You never want to DIY your book cover. An amateur cover design *will* affect your book's success. So be sure you know your genre and have done your market research, and that you hire the services of a professional book cover designer who understands your vision but also is in tune with what will speak to your ideal reader.

In my business, we sometimes work with clients who say they already have a cover design and therefore don't need this service included in their self-publishing package. In most cases what they mean is that they have either come up with a front cover design concept themselves, or they are friends with an artist or have someone on their team who has helped them come up with a design *concept*, which is usually limited to the front cover.

The problem, though, is that unless someone is a professional book cover designer, they are not always aware of what's trending in your genre, or knowledgeable about what elements and colors are proven to convert to sales, the scale and placement of graphics to text, and the spec requirements of the print-on-demand platform that will print and distribute the book.

Again, while it's okay to offer your designer a front cover concept as inspiration and to help capture your vision, I believe you'll have the most success when you allow your designer to do what they do best and create a few cover concepts themselves. If you still insist on coming up with the concept yourself, your designer can create a custom design based on that concept.

Also, having a front cover concept does not mean you do not need a professional book cover designer to lay out the full cover for print, or create the Kindle cover in the correct dimensions. Remember, the cover designer also sizes the final print-ready PDF that wraps the paperback—front, spine and back. The dimensions of that PDF depend on the book's trim size and the final page count of the formatted interior file. The width of the spine, bleed, etc. has to be exact in order for your cover to get accepted during the review process and to print properly.

Bottom line: be sure to include the cover design option in your self-publishing package or enlist the services of a professional cover designer who will offer a print-ready PDF cover for your paperback and a high-resolution e-book cover for digital publishing, as well as some 3D cover mockups for use in your marketing.

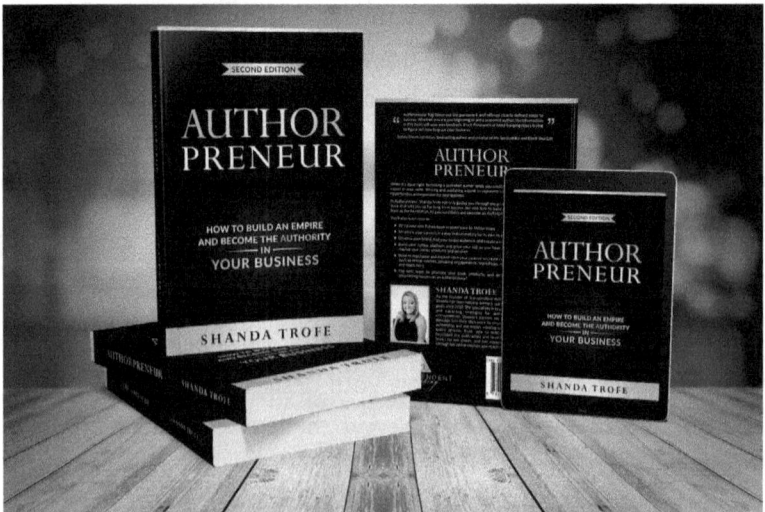

3D mockup for my book, Authorpeneur

Places to find a cover designer:

- Word-of-mouth – Ask other authors or check their copyright page for a credited name.

- 99designs – Have designers compete for the gig, for one set price you list before the contest begins.

- Fiverr – This option is hit-or-miss. Like many things in life, when it comes to the world of publishing, you often get what you pay for, so if you go this route be sure you find a top-level seller with stellar reviews.

- Freelance sites such as Upwork or Freelancer – just as above, you'll want to check their reviews and ask to see their portfolio.

- Self-Publishing Service Providers.

Paperback Formatting / Book Design

You want to ensure the same level of professionalism is used to create the interior of your book. That's achieved by carrying over the design and branding from the exterior, with a custom title page that matches the cover and by utilizing those fonts in the chapter titles and subheadings.

For this reason, I usually recommend outsourcing cover design and interior formatting to one service provider. This is easy to do when you engage a person or company that offers complete packages; however, if you find a cover designer that you like but perhaps doesn't offer interior formatting, be sure to find out which fonts were used on the cover so you can share that information with your book formatter. This is why it's a good idea to have the front cover created first.

If matching the interior to the exterior is not important to you and you're trying to cut costs but still come up with a professional design, you can use software such as Vellum (for Mac) or Atticus. Both have limited design features that allow you to at least format the interior in the proper dimensions and with the correct margins for publishing. Note: This may be an option for you if you are a bit tech-savvy and a fast learner, and your book doesn't include too many elements that would require more extensive formatting such as multiple tables, charts, photos/graphics, special fonts, etc. Also keep in mind that design software often comes with a cost, and for that cost you can usually outsource the design to a professional; however, if you plan to write and publish multiple books, it may be an investment to consider.

E-book Formatting

If you are working with a professional book formatter, they will supply the formatting for both the paperback and the e-book. With my clients, I recommend that we finalize the paperback's interior first, then use that file, which has already been polished and proofed, to create the .epub file. This way we are not making changes to two files simultaneously.

If, however, you are only publishing an e-book, you might try your hand at the formatting since it's not as robust as paperback formatting. If you are staying exclusive to Amazon, you could use Kindle Create, which is their free formatting tool. While it's not too difficult to use, it's important that your e-book have an interactive (hyperlinked) Table of Contents that takes readers to the coordinating section, as there are no page numbers in an e-book for the TOC to reference.

You'll also want to ensure that any other links in your e-book are hyperlinked to their coordinating website, and that you use clickable text instead of displaying the entire link.

It's also important to note that if you use Amazon's free formatting tool they are going to export that file as a .kmp file, which only works with KDP. That means if you are going wide with your e-book and would like it published on other platforms, you will still need a properly formatted .epub file. This is why I recommend hiring a professional book formatter who will offer an .epub version to upload to Amazon along with other retailers such as iBooks, Kobo and Barnes and Noble Press.

If you are going wide with your e-book, you can upload it to a digital publishing aggregator such as Draft2Digital and utilize their free e-book conversion tool. Once your e-book is converted to the proper file type, they will distribute it to all the main e-book retailers on your behalf and retain a small fee. Even if you go this route, I still recommend that you upload your e-book through KDP directly and then utilize Draft2Digital for the remaining retailers.

Success Tip: You can use Draft2Digital's formatting tool just to convert and export your e-book to an .epub file without turning on distribution—an easy way for you to get an .epub file if you don't want to spend the money on a formatter. Just keep in mind that Draft2Digital's free formatting service is limited to a few different styles to choose from, so if your book has graphics, tables, etc., your formatting will not be as high-end as with a professional book formatter. I would only recommend using this option when your book primarily has text.

CHAPTER 9

Publish Like a Pro

Understanding Print-on-Demand for Your Paperback

When it comes time to publish your paperback, you'll have plenty of print-on-demand options to choose from, so how do you decide? I like to work primarily with IngramSpark, KDP and/or Barnes & Noble Press for print-on-demand, and I'll go over each option briefly in this section. However, there are others you may want to research such as LuLu, Bookbaby and Blurb, to name a few.

With print-on-demand, you can upload your book's interior and cover files, add the metadata, choose the categories and price, and, once the files are approved, turn on distribution and have your book for sale via online retailers such as Amazon and Barnes and Noble in a matter of days, sometimes even hours.

Print-on-demand distributors pay you royalties on the net sales made via online retailers, which can be directly deposited to your bank account each month, though, as mentioned earlier, most pay on a sixty-day lag, so understand that you will usually wait a couple of months for your first royalty check.

Also recall that you can buy wholesale copies from your print-on-demand printer at a discounted rate to sell at your live events or on your website, and pocket the difference as profit. Thus, your print-on-demand platform becomes both your printer and the distributor of your paperback.

Choosing the Best Print-on-Demand Option for Your Book

Now that you understand how print-on-demand works, how do you choose which option is best for your self-published book?

I get asked this question a lot, and the answer always depends on your goals.

For example, if you simply want your paperback listed for sale on Amazon (where the majority of your online book sales will likely come from), and you want to be able to buy wholesale copies at a very low cost, then KDP (which is owned by Amazon) is a great print-on-demand option.

That said, KDP is also the choice with the least number of distribution options, unless you have an ISBN issued by Amazon and you select their expanded distribution option. However, I always recommend authors own their ISBNs (see my explanation for this in Chapter 6), so expanded distribution via KDP would not be an option in that case.

So let's say you went the KDP route but now you also want your book available for online sale via Barnes & Noble. Just as Amazon has KDP for print-on-demand, Barnes & Noble offers Barnes & Noble Press for self-publishing. Since you'll own your ISBN instead of using a free Amazon-owned ISBN, you simply upload your interior files via Barnes & Noble Press and—voila!—it's available there as well.

NOTE: If you decide to upload your paperback files to Barnes & Noble Press in addition to KDP, you'll need two separate cover files because they have slightly different formatting requirements. Be sure to let your cover designer know so they can prepare a print-ready PDF for each platform.

Authors who want their paperback to be available through the over 40,000 retailers in addition to Amazon and B&N.com should go with IngramSpark. Owned by Ingram Content Group, the world's largest book distributor, IngramSpark offers more distribution options than KDP and Barnes and Noble Press, including a desirable book returnability program. Most brick-and-mortar bookstores, especially large chain bookstores, are less likely to carry a book that's not returnable to the distributor if it doesn't sell, so if your goal is to get them to carry your book (extremely hard to do in today's competitive market, by the way), you need to keep this in mind when choosing your distributor.

In addition to having a buy-back plan in place, offering retailers a 55% wholesale discount is also helpful for the indie author who plans to pursue bookstores, libraries or universities, so, again, IngramSpark would be the best bet.

Now, that's not to say you can't sell your KDP published book through independent bookstores where *you* would supply the inventory yourself. I'm specifically talking about the larger stores such as Books-a-Million and Barnes & Noble's brick-and-mortar locations that prefer to order directly from the distributor. Some of the smaller bookstores will agree to carry your book, and they'll purchase inventory directly from the author or carry the book on consignment.

One thing to note: just because your book is available to over 40,000 retailers through IngramSpark doesn't mean those retailers will automatically carry the book. It's still up to the author to do the legwork in most cases; however, those retailers have a relationship with Ingram where they will buy the books directly so they can return them as needed. Of course, once you turn on distribution for your paperback with IngramSpark, they will also distribute your book to many online retailers—Amazon, B&N.com, Books-A-Million, Indigo, etc. You can find Ingram's distribution list on their website: www.IngramSpark.com.

There are pros and cons to each option, so only you can decide which is best for your self-published book. Just know that with KDP and Barnes & Noble Press, your cost per wholesale copy is usually slightly lower than with IngramSpark. If you prefer hardcover over paperback, I suggest that you go with IngramSpark since up until recently KDP only offered paperbacks for print, and their hardcover option is still in beta at the time of writing this book. While I have a few authors who desire hardcovers as well, most only publish their print books in paperback to keep their costs low and profit margin high.

What I do for most of my authors (depending on their goals) is first upload the paperback to IngramSpark and turn on distribution one to two weeks before the actual launch so that it has time to show up via online retailers. It typically shows up on Amazon rather quickly, while B&N.com can sometimes take longer to add the title and metadata when it's distributed through IngramSpark instead of uploading directly to B&N Press.

Success Tip: Once I see the paperback is listed on Amazon, I upload the paperback files to KDP as well and turn on distribution. This way, KDP will override IngramSpark for Amazon sales, so you will get paid directly through KDP for Amazon royalties instead of Ingram, which I find is usually slightly higher since through IngramSpark we are offering retailers such as Amazon a wholesale discount of 55%. This simply cuts out the middleman and it gives you the best of both worlds because you get the expanded distribution and book returnability through Ingram, while still benefiting from what KDP has to offer. Additionally, you'll now have two print-on-demand printers to choose from in which to purchase your author copies. I usually recommend ordering a copy from each and deciding which quality you like best for your book as they each tend to print slightly differently. I often find that while KDP has the lower price point for author copies, their quality is not as great as Ingram. However, I have some authors who prefer KDP over Ingram for author copies, so that's why I recommend ordering a copy from each.

I often get asked if each version of the paperback needs its own ISBN when uploading the files across multiple platforms such as IngramSpark, KDP and B&N Press. The answer is NO. You only need one ISBN for the paperback, and one interior paperback PDF that you will upload to each platform. However, if you plan to publish a hardcover in addition to the paperback, then the hardcover would need its own ISBN as it's a separate version of your book. Same with the audiobook.

Success Tip: When you upload the paperback to IngramSpark and add the book's details, they will ask for your publishing date and "on sale" date. If you set those dates to match the future date of your actual launch, the paperback will show up as a pre-order via online retailers such as Amazon and B&N once you turn on distribution. However, it's important to note that if you are also uploading your paperback to KDP as well, the presale information for the paperback will disappear once the paperback is published via KDP.

This is a nice feature since you won't be announcing the book until its actual launch date, so if someone were to find it online, you'd want it to say "available for pre-order" instead of "available." However, I don't recommend this as a selling strategy for pre-sales, meaning I don't recommend telling people the paperback is up for pre-order via online retailers since you'll want to wait to drive all traffic to Amazon on the date of your actual launch. I instead recommend hosting a pre-sale for author-signed copies from your own inventory of books that you'll order from the printer, sign, and ship to your customer yourself. You'll also earn more profits this way, which I'll explain in this chapter.

Uploading Your Paperback

KDP, Barnes & Noble Press, IngramSpark, or any other print-on-demand service will walk you through everything you need to enter as far as the book's details and metadata once it's time to upload your files. Most have quality customer service should you have a question along the way, but to set yourself up for success, here's a list of what you'll need so you're ready when the time comes.

- Title
- Subtitle
- Author Name
- Contributors' Names (if applicable)
- ISBN
- Imprint Name (see Chapter 6)
- Series Name (if applicable)
- Edition Number (only if not the first edition. If it's the first edition, leave blank)
- Categories/Sub-categories
- Seven Keyword Tags
- Book Blurb
- Author Bio
- Retail Price
- Trim Size
- Hardcover or Paperback (cover requirements are different for each)
- Binding (perfect bound for paperback)
- Paper (white or cream. I prefer white. If you select cream, make sure any graphics have a transparent background so they don't print with a white background on cream paper.)
- Page Count (of the final formatted interior PDF)
- Cover Finish (glossy or matte)

- Publishing Date and "On Sale" Date (IngramSpark)
- Print-ready PDF (of the formatted interior file with the proper trim size and margins)
- Print-ready PDF Cover (of the front, back and spine that wraps the book and is sized based on the final dimensions and page count of the interior file)

Once you upload the files and submit them to IngramSpark, they will go into review. Assuming there are no issues, you will receive an email, usually within one to three days, announcing that the e-proof is ready for review. At that point, you can log into IngramSpark, view the e-proof on your computer, and order a printed copy.

To order a printed copy, however, you must first approve the e-proof. I highly recommend approving it "for orders from this account only"—this way, you will not turn on distribution right away. You'll always want to order a physical copy to review in print before you turn on distribution, because once you turn it on, IngramSpark will begin sending your book's information to online retailers to be listed for sale or pre-order.

Once you receive a printed copy and you are happy with it, turn on distribution a week or two before your launch date to ensure the online retailers have time to list your book for sale on their marketplace before your launch. As mentioned earlier, in my experience the book will show up as a pre-order on Amazon in a matter of days but it can take B&N.com a bit longer to add it.

Success Tip: Sometimes B&N is slow to add the cover and all the book's metadata once they list the book for sale. To expedite the process, reach out to titles@bn.com with the ISBN, cover, author bio, and book blurb and ask them to update your listing once your title shows up on their site.

Once the paperback shows up on Amazon via IngramSpark, now you can upload the files to KDP. You'll upload the files and add the metadata as you did with IngramSpark; the only difference with KDP is that you won't have the opportunity to put the paperback up for pre-order (only the e-book).

NOTE: KDP and IngramSpark also have different cover requirements. While a KDP-sized cover will get accepted by IngramSpark, an IngramSpark-sized cover will not get accepted by KDP. Either way, it's a good idea to get separate covers sized specifically to each platform's requirements so that they each print properly.

Wholesale Author Copies vs. Proof Copies

Another difference between KDP and IngramSpark is that with IngramSpark, once you approve the e-proof, you are able to order "author copies" which are your wholesale copies at the discounted rate. These do not have any indication printed on them that they are proof copies, so they are available for resale. At this point, you could technically order hundreds of books if you'd like, but I don't recommend placing a large book order until you order a copy to see it in print first.

With KDP, you have the option to order a "proof copy" before you submit the book for publishing, but please note, the proof copies from KDP come with a band printed across the front that says "not for resale." You may order up to five proof copies from KDP before you submit the book for publishing, but once you submit the book, it will go into review for approximately twenty-four hours before the paperback is available for sale via Amazon (upon approval). There is no option to "enable orders from this account only" as there is with IngramSpark. Once you submit the book to KDP, it will go live upon approval, whereas you actually turn distribution on via IngramSpark.

Success Tip: As you can see, you're going to want to allow plenty of time to order a physical copy from both IngramSpark and KDP, and allow time for those copies to be printed and shipped before your launch, so it's a good idea not to wait until the last minute to upload your files. Once you receive your printed copy, if you're happy with it, then you can place an order to have on hand for your actual launch date or to fill any orders from your pre-order of author-signed copies, and you'll need to allow ample time for that larger order as well.

Host a Pre-Sale for Signed Copies

Self-publishing a high-quality book requires an investment. The cost of professional editing, formatting, and cover design adds up, in addition to your marketing budget and expenses to build your author platform. One way to offset some of your publishing investment is to host a pre-sale for signed copies of your paperback once your files are uploaded to the printer, but before you turn on distribution and launch your book via online retailers.

The idea is that you'll purchase your author copies at the whole-sale rate directly from your print-on-demand printer (I recommend IngramSpark for this since, as mentioned, you can order wholesale author copies before turning on distribution) and resell them to your friends, family, mailing list, and social media community at the retail rate, which allows you to keep the difference in profits.

Let's say, hypothetically, that your paperback costs you approximately $4 per copy to print. While you'll have to pay for shipping to receive your author copies from the printer, you'll still make a nice profit when you resell it for the retail price at your own efforts (e.g., website, social media, mailing list, live events).

So, if your retail price were set at $16, and after including your shipping costs to receive the books, that brings your price per copy from $4 to $6, you're still making $10 per copy for every pre-order you receive. If you received 100 pre-orders, that would net you approximately $1,000! Even if you sold half of that and brought in 50 pre-orders, that's still $500 that you'd have upfront, which would fund your initial book order, and leave a nice profit.

You're probably wondering: what about the cost to then ship the signed copies of my book to my customers?

Well, you have two options:

1. You can calculate shipping for each order and ask the customer to pay the shipping cost. This is not what I recommend because many people have a Prime membership with Amazon, so they may decide to instead wait until the book is available via online retailers to purchase a copy. While you'll still earn income when your paperback is purchased online, usually, the royalty you'll receive for online orders is far less than the profits you'll retain through selling copies from your own inventory.

2. Add a few dollars to your regular retail price and tell your customers that the pre-sale price includes tax and shipping (what I recommend). The extra dollars you've added will cover that, plus any sales tax you may owe to your state (you'll need to talk to your tax professional about collecting and paying sales tax in your state).

Tips for Success:

- Be sure your final interior and cover files are uploaded and approved by your print-on-demand printer and that you've ordered at least one printed copy to review before you begin your pre-sale.

- You'll need a way to collect the funds and shipping addresses from your customers. This can easily be done by creating a PayPal button (you can either embed the HTML code on your website wherever you'd like the button to appear, or you may opt to share the button's link directly). When creating your button, be sure to tick the box where you'll require the shipping address for purchase. You'll also need a PayPal Business account for this, if you don't already have one.

- When you share your pre-order, you'll want to include a photo of the book's cover, the blurb/description, and the pre-sale information. Here's some sample text you're welcome to use:

> I'm now accepting pre-orders for author-signed copies of my upcoming book, [insert title], for a flat rate of $___. This price includes tax and shipping within the continental US. Please contact me for international orders: [insert email address].

All pre-orders will be shipped on publication day, tentatively scheduled for [insert launch date]. Please allow 5-7 days for delivery once shipped.

Learn more: [insert shortened book blurb]

Pre-order your copy here: [insert payment link]

Some authors include a free gift to make the pre-sale even more enticing. This can be something as simple as a bookmark, pen, or handmade gift.

Success Tip: If you're only including the book inside the package and nothing more, consider using the Media Mail option available via USPS to reduce shipping costs.

Create a finite time for your pre-order since most people will wait until the last minute to order. I usually recommend running a pre-sale for 7-10 days, and sending out and posting several reminders in the days leading up to the pre-sale's close.

Once you close your pre-sale, you'll know exactly how many author copies to order, and you'll have the funds available for your first book order, plus a nice profit.

Be sure to allow ample time for printing and shipping to receive your author copies from the printer and to allow time to sign and package the books for your customers. You should have your orders signed, packaged, and ready to go by publication day, so it's a good idea to launch your pre-sale for author-signed copies at least a month before your paperback goes live via online retailers.

Uploading the E-book

If you're offering Amazon exclusivity of your e-book by enrolling in KDP Select, you'll upload your e-book files to KDP only and tick the box indicating that you'd like to enroll in the KDP Select program, which runs in ninety-day increments. Just be advised that your enrollment will automatically renew for an additional ninety days unless you opt out before your initial enrollment period ends.

However, if you're going wide with your e-book, meaning you'll be distributing it across multiple retailers, then I recommend you first upload the files to KDP; however, in this case you will not enroll in the KDP Select program because you won't be offering Amazon exclusivity. Once the e-book is uploaded to KDP, you can then upload it elsewhere such as Draft2Digital or Smashwords, which are e-book aggregator services that will distribute your e-book across multiple platforms on your behalf for a small percentage, or you can upload the files to each platform individually such as Barnes & Noble Press, Kobo, iBooks, etc.

Either way, you'll always want to distribute the e-book through KDP and upload the files there yourself so that you have more control over your Amazon listing, which you'll need if you plan to do the Amazon bestseller launch, which I'll cover in the next chapter.

Things you'll need before you upload your e-book files:

- Title
- Subtitle
- Author Name

- Contributors' Names (if applicable)
- ISBN (one that's exclusive to the e-book. ISBNs are optional for e-books published on KDP but I recommend having one if you're going wide with your e-book as it will be needed for some of the other platforms. You'll use the same e-book ISBN across all platforms, but it will need to be different from your paperback ISBN)
- Imprint Name (see Chapter 6)
- Series Name (if applicable)
- Edition Number (if not the first edition)
- Categories/Sub-categories (two for KDP, but you'll have the opportunity to add up to ten categories by opening a ticket with KDP)
- Seven Keyword Tags
- Book Blurb
- Retail Price
- E-book File (.epub)
- Front Kindle Cover (1,600 x 2,560 pixels in TIFF or JPEG format)

One perk KDP offers for e-books that they don't currently offer for paperback is the option to schedule a pre-order. You can list your e-book for pre-order for a full year leading up to the publication date. However, here are some things to keep in mind that, unfortunately, some authors learn the hard way:

- If you change the retail price of your e-book while it's up for pre-order, you'll lose the royalty you would have earned at the original price point for any pre-orders received up to that point. For instance, let's say you had your e-book up for pre-order for three months leading up to your launch at the $2.99 price point, and the day before your launch you switched the price to $0.99, you would lose the 70% royalty on any $2.99 pre-order sales you received for those three months, and you'd instead earn 35% of $0.99 for *all* pre-orders.

- You can begin a pre-order without uploading the actual .epub file. This offers you additional time to complete the e-book while your book is up for pre-order. You'd simply upload the cover, book description and pertinent information so the Amazon listing could be created; however, KDP will lock you out of the option to upload your e-book file seventy-two hours before the launch, so if you don't have your file uploaded in time you'll have a problem on your hands. There will be no way to upload your e-book, and they will cancel all of your pre-order sales, which means you'll lose all of that pre-order income, so be sure not to miss that deadline.

- Worse yet, if you can't make your publishing date and you have to cancel your pre-order, KDP will suspend your ability to host a pre-order for *a full year*. They will sometimes offer a one-time forgiveness if you contact them and explain the error, so if this happens to you, be sure to give it a try. Again, they will not offer forgiveness twice.

CHAPTER 10

Launching Your Bestseller

Your e-book and paperback files are uploaded and you've done everything to prepare for the launch, and now you're filled with excitement (and likely a fair amount of nervousness) about sending your book out into the world. However, as I mentioned earlier, what you don't want to do is just hit publish and wait for the sales to come rolling in. That is unrealistic and unfortunately what some authors believe will make their book dreams come true. You know better, though, because you're a savvy authorpreneur, so you're going to launch your book like a pro, and in this chapter, I'm going to share how to do just that.

At the time of writing this book, I've launched over five hundred Amazon #1 bestselling books for my clients, and have taught countless students and independent publishers how to do it themselves through my online programs. I have a proven system that works, to not only get your book to bestseller, but to also earn you plenty of reviews and get your book noticed by Amazon. I've done many types of launches over the years, and I've tweaked this system along the way, but these are the steps that, to date, work best—at least in my experience.

One main reason to set up a proper launch, outside of earning reviews and becoming a bestselling author, is so you get on Amazon's radar and ignite their algorithm. If you can do that, then Amazon may begin cross-promoting your book to their customers, and trust me, you want Amazon pushing your books!

If you're a customer who peruses Amazon for books to read, then I'm sure you've received emails that say: "Based on your recent search, we thought you'd enjoy these books." Let's say you click on one of those books from the email and you're taken to that book's product page on Amazon. If you scroll down, you might see, "Customers who bought this book also bought," with a variety of similar books featured. Or, "Products related to this item," and "Books you may like," with more books featured. Keep scrolling and you may see, "Customers who viewed this item also viewed," where you'll find even more books that are similar to the one you originally clicked on.

Have you ever wondered how Amazon decides which books to feature in those spots?

Well, that's Amazon's powerful algorithm at work, showing you books they think you'll purchase based on your recent activity. With millions of books on their website, they don't do that for every author. So, how can you get Amazon to feature your book to their customers? One of the best ways to get on their radar is to get your book listed on not only the Bestsellers lists but the New Releases lists as well. The way you do that is with a strategic book launch.

Note: Unlike the Bestsellers lists, you can only rank on the New Releases list during the first thirty days of publishing.

Selecting Your Keywords

Before you launch your book you're going to want to do your keyword research as we briefly discussed in Chapter 8. There are many ways to do this, such as with special software like Publisher Rocket that will let you know the following information for each keyword or keyword phrase you are considering:

- Number of competitors
- Number of monthly searches on Amazon
- Number of monthly searches on Google
- Competitive score
- Monthly Amazon earnings

This is one of the tools I use to conduct research for my clients' launches, but if you don't want to invest in special software, you can, as mentioned earlier, research for free by typing your main keywords into the Amazon search bar (make sure you are searching under the "Books" or "Kindle" category) and noting the keywords and keyword phrases Amazon populates in their drop-down menu.

For instance, let's say you were writing a book on the keto diet. If you first select "Books" to the left of the search bar, then type in your main keyword, keto, you'll notice a list of keywords and keyword phrases that auto-populate from the dropdown menu:

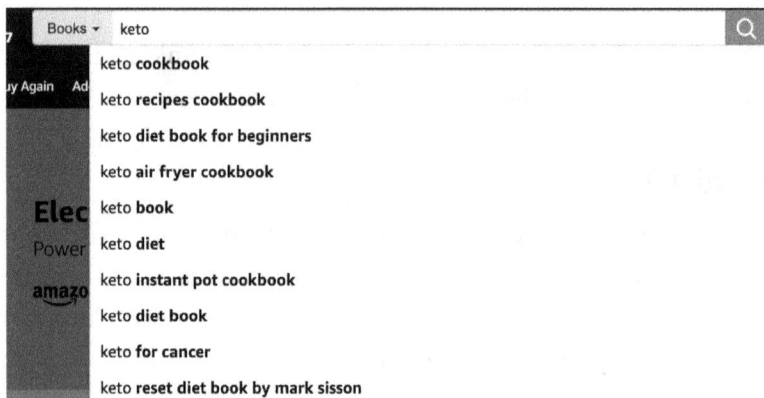

| Books ▾ | keto | 🔍 |

keto **cookbook**

keto **recipes cookbook**

keto **diet book for beginners**

keto **air fryer cookbook**

keto **book**

keto **diet**

keto **instant pot cookbook**

keto **diet book**

keto **for cancer**

keto **reset diet book by mark sisson**

You should do this with all keywords and phrases that pertain to your book's topic. Following the example above, you might also search for keto diet to return additional results:

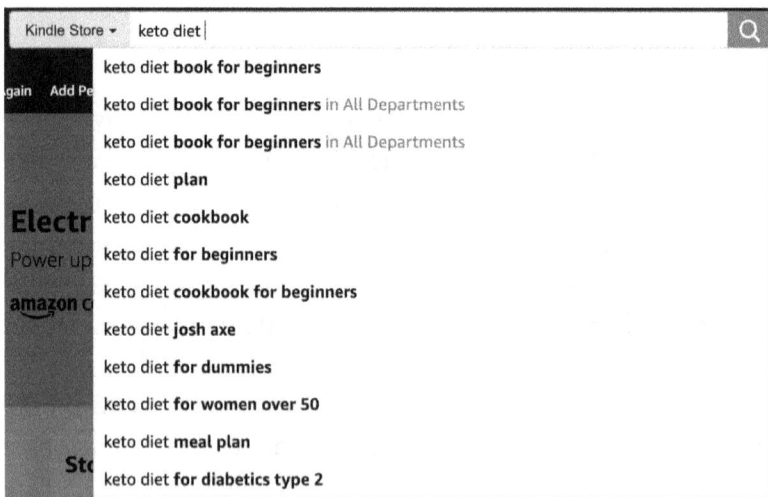

| Kindle Store ▾ | keto diet | 🔍 |

keto diet **book for beginners**

keto diet **book for beginners** in All Departments

keto diet **book for beginners** in All Departments

keto diet **plan**

keto diet **cookbook**

keto diet **for beginners**

keto diet **cookbook for beginners**

keto diet **josh axe**

keto diet **for dummies**

keto diet **for women over 50**

keto diet **meal plan**

keto diet **for diabetics type 2**

This is an easy way to discover what your ideal reader is searching for on Amazon in relation to books on your topic. Now you can take some of those keywords/phrases and incorporate them into your book's metadata.

How many keywords/keyword phrases do you need? You'll want to ensure your book's product listing is optimized for SEO, so decide on a title and subtitle, with one of them also incorporating your most powerful keyword. Also, sprinkle some keywords in your book description, and have on hand your seven hidden keyword tags that KDP asks for when you are creating the book's product listing.

Scheduling the Promo

Next, you'll want to decide on a promotional period for your launch. These can last anywhere from one to seven days, but for my clients, I prefer a three- to five-day launch. This is a dedicated time when we'll drop the price of the e-book to free or $.99, and drive traffic to get downloads while utilizing the author's book launch team to gain reviews and additional downloads. Remember, your goal is to reach bestseller on Amazon, and this is why you want to utilize the Kindle edition—it's easier to get a large number of downloads on a discounted e-book than a full-priced paperback. Even if you're going wide and distributing your e-book on other platforms, the focus for this promotional period should be Amazon.

The high number of downloads within a short time boosts your e-book's sales ranking in your categories, and since you'll have your book listed in up to ten categories (which I'll explain in a moment), you'll have the potential to reach bestseller in several, which means more eyes on your book, and more places for Amazon to consider for cross-promotion.

At the time of writing this book, those of us who facilitate bestseller launches are noticing a lag in Amazon updating the sales ranking. The ranking should update hourly, but for reasons unknown, whether it be a glitch or a change in the algorithm, launches that used to take one day to reach bestseller status can now take up to three days. That's why I've recently switched from doing three-day launches to hosting five-day launches for my clients, with a heavy emphasis on book promotions during the first three days, but with paid features scheduled for all five days.

So decide on a five-day period in which you'll launch your book (I like to launch Thursday-Monday), and whether your e-book will be free or $.99 during this time.

Free or $.99 Promotion?

Deciding how to price your e-book during the launch depends largely on how you are choosing to distribute it. If you elect to enroll your book in the KDP Select exclusivity program, you'll receive five free promo days for every ninety days you're enrolled, and during those days you can discount the Kindle edition to free. However, as mentioned early on, this means you must offer Amazon exclusivity during your launch. If you are going wide and distributing your e-book across other platforms, Amazon will not allow you to price it under $.99, so you'll need to do a five-day $.99 promotional period instead.

Another thing to keep in mind as you make your decision is that there is both a free and paid Kindle store. If you drop your e-book to free for five days you'll end up with far more downloads, but your book will rank at bestseller in the free Kindle store as opposed to the paid Kindle store, where, outside of your promotional period, it will be competing for sales ranking.

To get your book to rank at bestseller in the paid Kindle store, it's helpful to have a large mailing list and social media following, along with a strong book launch team who will agree to download a copy of your Kindle edition for $.99 before they post their review.

As mentioned above, usually $.99 launches result in far fewer downloads than free ones; however, that's not to say you can't get it to bestseller with a $.99 launch and little to no social following. One way to do this is to engage bargain book promoters, who will agree to advertise your book to their audiences for a fee. You'll just need to schedule several features for day one of your launch, and be sure you've placed your e-book into categories with low competition.

There are pros and cons for each style of launch, so only you can decide which is best for your book. I will say one of the things I love about free launches is that I can average between one thousand and three thousand downloads of an e-book during that time; plus, since my books and my clients' books always offer a free gift inside, it often results in numerous new subscribers joining our mailing lists, especially if we have an awesome freebie.

Success Tip: Sometimes I have an author who doesn't want to announce that their e-book is free during its launch but still wants to run the free promotion to get it to bestseller quickly. In this case, we will do both a free and $.99 launch strategy, meaning we schedule a free promo for the three days leading up to the launch, and raise it to $.99 for the launch itself. This can result in the best of both worlds: hitting bestseller in both the free Kindle store and the paid Kindle store. Let me explain.

The author would only tell their book launch team about the free period (and ask them to download a copy before posting their review) while at the same time utilizing the paid book promotion features mentioned above. Then, after the free days end, the e-book will be listed at $.99 and they'll launch it publicly to their mailing list and on social media; at this point we would also have some additional features set up with book promoters who feature $.99 e-books. The number of downloads from their own marketing efforts, coupled with some paid features with book promoters, will boost their sales ranking in the paid Kindle store as well, often to bestseller.

NOTE: It's important to note that there are different book promoters for free launches and paid launches, so be sure to do your research and schedule each accordingly. A Google search for "Bargain Book Promotions" should return plenty of results.

Selecting Your Book's Categories

At this point you may be wondering how many downloads you'll need to reach bestseller. There is no way to know for sure, even with software like Publisher Rocket that tells you how many sales the number one book in your category has sold in a day's time to reach that position. That information is only accurate at the time of reviewing those numbers. The reason is that Amazon's bestsellers lists update on an hourly basis, and you have no way of knowing what other authors in your categories have planned for the day of your launch, or what promotions other published books that you're up against have scheduled for that day.

What you can do is strategically select categories that are, first and foremost, relevant to your topic but also those you have the best chance of ranking in. This means not selecting broad categories with high competition. Let's revisit the Keto Diet example from earlier. If you were writing that book, you may be inclined to select the main category of **Health, Fitness & Dieting**. However, that broad category has over 50,000 books, so you might select a subcategory of that parent category, where there's lower competition, such as **Diets & Weight Loss** (still over 50,000 books in this sub-category). So, you can even take it a step further and find a subcategory of **Diets,** which is more niched and offers even lower competition—at the time of writing this book, only 2,000 books. If you keep going, you'll find that under the Diets category, there is both a **Ketogenic Diet** (32 books) and **Low Carb Diet** (only 26 books) category. Score!

There are numerous subcategories on Amazon, and some of them are not visible when it comes time to publish and select your categories inside the KDP dashboard. While you can find some of the subcategories by searching the book and Kindle categories on Amazon, you may want to use special software such as KDP Rocket or Bestseller Ranking Pro to narrow down your research.

Compiling a Book Launch Team

Two to three weeks before the launch, you'll want to compile your book launch team. This team is made up of a group of readers who will agree to review an ARC (Advanced Reader Copy) of your book, usually in PDF format, and then leave a review on Amazon during its launch. Authors always ask me how many members they need on their team. My answer: the more, the better! But if you can only get a handful of reviewers, that's better than nothing, because social proof will help with your future book sales. It's been estimated that for every hundred books you sell, just one person will take the time to leave a review organically, so it's important to compile a team for this task so your book earns plenty of reviews during its launch. When you see an author with lots of reviews on their book, that usually means they had a strong book launch team in place.

For my books, I usually aim for a launch team of twenty to twenty-five people. I could easily get more, but I don't want to exhaust all of my resources, meaning I want to have an audience left to market my book to! If they are getting a free PDF copy of my book for being on the team, they may decide not to purchase a copy, so be strategic when deciding how much of your mailing list or community you'll include in this process.

Success Tip: A handful of reviews typically get blocked or rejected during every launch, so if you'd like twenty reviews, invite twenty-five people to be on your team. If you'd like a hundred reviews, ask a hundred and ten, and so on. Sometimes Amazon rejects a review for no apparent rhyme or reason (and they will not reveal their reasoning either), so it's best not to dwell on it or bother contacting Amazon and just focus on how to get other reviews.

NOTE: While, as mentioned, we don't always know why a review is rejected, we do know it's against Amazon's terms of service to ask friends and family to review the book; therefore, if they connect the reviewer to you in any way they may block or remove that review. Of course, authors sometimes ask friends and family anyway, but don't bother asking anyone to be on your team who has the same last name as you, shares the same computer or shipping address, or anyone you've sent a gift to from within your Amazon account in the past. Also, to be eligible to leave a review, the reviewer must have spent $50 on Amazon in the past twelve months. This ensures that people don't set up fake accounts to post reviews.

A great place to find reviewers to be on your launch team is inside author groups or masterminds, or among your colleagues. If you're still coming up short, you can use a service such as Pubby, Booksprout or NetGalley. Please be advised, you must never pay for a review as it's against Amazon's terms of service and could get your account shut down, but these services have an ethical way for you to earn reviews which is not considered paying for it. You are instead paying a membership fee to join their platform where you can ask members to read and review your book (for free). Booksprout offers both a free and paid option, with the paid option offering a bit more protection against piracy. In my experience, Pubby works better than Booksprout for non-fiction, and Net-Galley is not my favorite.

Scheduling the Launch

Now that you have your book launch team in place and they are reviewing your ARC two to three weeks out from the launch, it's time to plan the actual launch. You'll want to submit your e-book for publishing at least a week in advance of the launch date, because you'll need the link to the book's Amazon page before you can schedule your paid features with those bargain book promoters I mentioned earlier.

Success Tip: If you are doing a $.99 launch, approximately one week before the launch, select a handful of reviewers from your book launch team to go to Amazon and post their review. For this to happen, your book must be fully published, not just available for pre-order—and this is one of the reasons that we publish *before* the launch. Some of the discounted book promoters require your book to have reviews, usually five or ten, before you can schedule paid features. Many of the features get booked out a week in advance (at least), so you're going to want to offer yourself enough time to schedule your promotions in order to get the date you want.

For example, if your launch date is April 1 you want to schedule your promotional launch period from April 1 – 5. You would submit the e-book for publishing at least a week prior, let's say March 24, which means it would be live on Amazon by the 25th. On that day you'll have a handful of your reviewers download a copy and leave their review (downloading a copy first will earn their review the Amazon Verified Purchase badge, although it's not necessary in order to leave a review). Next, grab the link to the book's product page on Amazon and schedule your paid features.

On April 1, day one of your launch period, you'll instruct your remaining launch team to go to Amazon, download a copy, and post their review. You should have your strongest paid features set up for day one of the launch, because remember, it's the number of downloads you get in a short time period that boosts your sales ranking.

NOTE: Don't panic if your launch team has said they've left their reviews and you don't see them on Amazon. Most reviews take up to seventy-two hours to post.

You'll also want to announce that your book is now available to your mailing list and via social media. Post plenty of times over your launch period, across all platforms.

If you've set up some powerful paid features with bargain book promoters, and managed your launch team successfully, then you should see your e-book begin to rank in the Kindle store. Scroll midway down your book's product page on Amazon and they will display up to three of the categories you are ranking in. Then you can click on the clickable blue subcategory, which is a hyperlink that will take you directly to the bestseller list for the category.

NOTE: it will take you to the paid Kindle store by default. If you are doing a free launch, you'll need to toggle over to the free Kindle store here:

119

Since Amazon only lists three places where your e-book is ranking at any given time, you'll need to manually search through your parent categories and the subcategories in the Kindle store to find your e-book on the other bestsellers lists (found listed down the left side of the page).

Be sure to take a screenshot of your book placing at #1 for each list. This is critically important, so pay close attention and grab those screenshots while your book is ranking because there will be no place to find it once the book's off the bestseller list.

If you are doing the $.99 promotion instead of the free promotion, and your book is ranking at bestseller in the paid Kindle Store, Amazon will add the bestseller badge to your book's listing while it is ranking at #1.

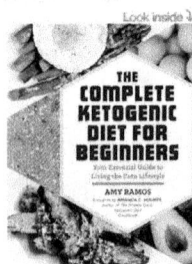

Next, you'll want to share your success on social media! Add a bestseller badge to your book cover for marketing images, and share it along with screenshots of your book ranking at #1. You're now a bestselling author with a bestselling book, and this will help with your marketing, which is where the real work begins. Don't worry, though, we'll cover that in the next chapter.

For the remaining days of your launch, keep driving downloads even after you've reached bestseller so your ranking doesn't tank drastically. Yes, it's important to get on Amazon's radar, but you don't just want to launch it to bestseller and then stop marketing efforts once you reach number one. This is why I now prefer a five-day launch, so I can have some features scheduled for days four and five as well, while the e-book is still free or $.99.

Success Tip: Repeat this process every few months through scheduled quarterly promotions where you drop it back down to free or $.99 for a few days. This will reignite the algorithm and earn you a bunch of downloads on your e-book, which means new readers and often new email subscribers and clients as well.

USA Today Bestseller Launches

For *USA Today* bestseller launches, I partner with someone who specializes in launches for large publications. These are for my clients who desire to hit a prestigious list as a way to up their credibility, gain massive exposure for their book, or increase their speaking fees. Note: If you're interested in hitting *USA Today*, you'll want to discount your e-book to $.99 and get a minimum of 3,000 downloads within a seven-day period, across various platforms, with a minimum of 500 of those sales coming from outside of Amazon to be eligible. It's also important to note that your e-book will need an ISBN so that Nielsen BookScan can track those sales across all platforms.

For these launches, I upload the author's e-book directly to KDP, Barnes & Noble Press, and sometimes Kobo. I optimize the keywords and categories as I would with an Amazon launch, but then it takes an incredible amount of advertising to ensure the e-book not only gets the required number of downloads in a one-week period but hits that benchmark of sales outside Amazon. As most people purchase from Amazon by default, it's helpful to partner with someone who has the means to ensure that happens through a massive mailing list and segregated advertising that drives Barnes & Noble sales in addition to Amazon sales. Because of this, these launches require a high five-figure investment to cover the cost of advertising. It won't be an ideal launch strategy for every author, but if you have the means and desire to earn the prestige that comes from hitting one of these lists, it can be very worthwhile.

Whichever path you choose, after your launch period ends, it's important to maintain ongoing marketing efforts for as long as your book is available for sale in order to keep it on Amazon's radar and in front of your ideal readers, which brings us to the next step in your authorship journey...

CHAPTER 11

Post-Launch Marketing

You thought writing the book was the hard part... and then comes the marketing.

Never fear, I have good news for you: *Marketing does not have to be hard.* It always seems daunting when an author doesn't know what to do or where to begin, but I'm going to break it down for you in this chapter so you'll hit the ground running once your book is published.

The first thing to realize is that marketing is a necessary and ongoing task for every author—at least those who want to realize their book's greatest potential and fulfill the goals I discussed over the previous chapters. Just as it was up to you to sit down and write the book, it's up to you and you alone to ensure that it stays in front of your target audience. Sure, you can hire a PR firm to help you, but in my experience that can be expensive and not entirely effective. Also, it's usually a contract for a finite amount of time, so eventually, you're going to have to learn to market your book yourself.

You're going to meet the most success as an author when you embrace marketing as part of your authorship journey—you know, the one that started out with you wanting to share your creativity, expertise and message with as many people who can benefit from it as possible. If you've followed the guidance in this book, you've created a high-quality book you can be proud of and launched it strategically to start the wheels in motion. Well, the next, and longest, leg of that journey is keeping the momentum going for years to come.

Early on in my publishing career, I had a client who hired me to help self-publish her book. We did everything to set it up for success: we ensured the content was great and spoke to her ideal reader; it had multiple levels of editing and proofreading to ensure the content was engaging and polished; we created a cover that aligned with what was trending in her genre; and launched it to bestseller to ignite Amazon's algorithm. She was off to the races!

Six months later, I received an email from her. She declared she was done writing books, and that her book was a failure and nobody was interested in it. It must've been an awful book, she said, because she wasn't receiving the sales she'd expected.

How could that be? I wondered. We'd done everything to set her up for success, or so I thought.

So, I started asking questions...

What have you done to keep your book in front of your ideal reader?

Have you run any advertising or hosted any promotions?

How many interviews have you done to keep your message in front of your target audience?

How often are you sharing valuable content in your area of expertise?

Have you become a contributor to share your expertise where your ideal readers are hanging out?

Where have you spoken on your topic?

How have you grown your social media following?

Do you run a Facebook group?

Are you still building and growing your mailing list?

Where are you delivering video content and articles?

Are you blogging, podcasting, creating content for YouTube?

The answer to all of those questions was NO. I was a bit dumb-founded. How in the world could this author think her book was a failure when she had literally done nothing to keep it in front of her ideal reader or continue to grow and nurture her author platform? How did she expect to earn sales if nobody knew about her book to begin with? There are millions of books on Amazon, after all. Did she really think we could just launch her book and then she could sit back and collect royalties for months on end?

And then I realized: I had failed her. While I had helped her self-publish her book and launch it to the world as she had hired me to do, I didn't educate her on the next steps post-publication. And that's what inspired me to begin creating content for authors by offering online courses, writing books, articles, and video content, and nurturing my community.

Even though our contract had ended after the book was published and launched, as the expert, I have a responsibility to my clients and readers to deliver valuable content. So, in the same way I'm showing up to write this book for you and create ongoing training so you don't make the same mistakes as my client, I am going to ask you to show up for yourself and put in the work.

I can teach you *what* to do to market your book, but I can't do it for you. Again, this is an ongoing journey for every author. But if you are proud of your book and believe in your message, then it is one you can learn to enjoy and have fun with—especially when you start receiving your royalty checks, see your mailing list grow, and gain new clients, all because you are out there sharing your message. When that begins to happen, you won't want to stop, so let's create a plan of action for you now to set you up for long-term success.

23 Ways to Market Your Book Post-Publication

Below I have listed twenty-three things you can do once your book is launched to keep it in front of your target audience:

1. **Run Amazon ads.** This is the first thing I advise you to do once your book is launched. If you don't like the thought of book marketing, running Amazon ads may be your

savior. Why? Because Amazon ads, when done right, can be highly effective as long as you have an enticing blurb and a high-quality cover. Without those two things, don't waste your time or money because the ads won't convert. But if you've followed what I've taught you here, you *will* have a high-quality book that's designed to convert to sales. After that, either invest in a program to learn how to run Amazon ads the right way, or hire a professional to do it for you. With Amazon ads, you are engaging in pay-per-click advertising and bidding on keywords that your ideal reader may be searching for. You can pay for placement, which means your book will come up in searches depending on the keywords in which your ideal reader is searching. You can also target your competitors' books, so your book shows up in searches when someone searches for a competitor's name or book title. Amazon ads are powerful, especially if you don't have time to do much else to market your book (although I don't recommend you stop here).

2. **Run Facebook ads to target your ideal reader.** While I favor Amazon ads over Facebook ads, they are still a great way to get your book in front of your ideal reader. This is another area you're not going to want to go into blindly, so either invest in a course or hire a professional to run these ads for you. With FB you will be targeting your ideal reader and paying when your ad is viewed or clicked, depending upon whether you are optimizing for impressions or for clicks.

3. **Upgrade to an author profile on Goodreads.** While many will argue that Goodreads is for readers and not

for authors, it's always a good idea to upgrade from your reader profile to an author profile and claim your book. You even have the option to add your book to the platform pre-publication leading up to your launch if you'd like.

4. **Apply for a BookBub "Featured Deal."** You'll want to create an author profile with BookBub and claim your book as the author, and then apply for a Featured Deal to try to get your book featured to their millions of subscribers. If you don't get selected, you can run Bookbub ads until it's time to apply again (30 days if submitting at the same price point). If your book does get selected for a Featured Deal, you'll pay a considerable fee to be featured, but their high number of subscribers (varies by genre) usually makes it well worth the investment. You can view their current fees and subscriber breakdown here: https://www.bookbub.com/partners/pricing

5. **Contact podcast hosts to schedule interviews.** In 2021, there were 850,000 active podcasts, with over 48 million total episodes, which shows a 20%+ increase over 2020[13]. Clearly, people love to absorb content in this way. Visit popular podcast directories such as iTunes and Stitcher, and do a search for shows on your area of expertise. When pitching a podcast host, be sure to listen to a few of their past episodes so you can personalize your pitch and let them know how much you enjoy their podcast and why you would be a good fit. Review the topics they've had in the past, and come up with one to three fresh interview

---

[13] https://nealschaffer.com/podcast-statistics/

topics with your own unique hook—one that will benefit their audience.

Success Tip: The fact that you wrote a book and you're now an author is *not* the pitch. Your goal is to get in front of your ideal reader and establish yourself as an expert. So ask yourself, what can I offer that will benefit this podcast's listeners? Pitch that idea to the host. Save the bit about your book for the end of the podcast when the host offers you an opportunity to share how listeners can get in touch with you. You can also mention that you are the bestselling author of your bestselling book in your bio that will be shared in the show notes and when the host introduces you.

6. **Pitch journalists for article mentions.** Same as above, you'll want to do your research and get to know what kind of content they share so you can personalize your pitch. Remember, the fact that you have a book will lend you credibility, but it's not your pitch. You want to share valuable content in your area of expertise and establish yourself as the expert. If the audience resonates with you, they'll find your book once they come seeking you out for more information.

7. **Approach local news stations for media appearances.** Many authors are intimidated by this and don't even bother trying, but the truth is getting featured by the local media is easier than you think. I have a few authors who are regular guests on their local news stations' morning show. Those morning shows are always looking for experts to feature, and here's a tip: Find a national day that coincides with your book, and offer to be interviewed on

the topic. For instance, let's say you wrote a book on your journey with breast cancer. Since October is National Breast Cancer Awareness Month, you could pitch your local news station to have you come on as a guest expert and be interviewed.

8. **Ask local bookstores to carry your book.** With the decline of brick-and-mortar bookstores amidst the rise of published authors, bookshelf space is highly competitive, but that doesn't mean bookstores in your area won't be open to supporting a local author. As mentioned, the large chain bookstores such as Barnes & Noble and Books-a-Million will want to order directly from the distributor, so to pitch those stores be sure your book is distributed by Ingram, is returnable, and offers retailers a 55% wholesale discount. The smaller independent stores will usually get inventory directly from the author, either at a discounted wholesale rate or through a consignment arrangement.

9. **Create a book funnel.** This is ideal for turning your readers into clients by getting them into your sales funnel where you can offer your other products or services. This can be done by selling a PDF copy of your e-book or offering your paperback for free and only charging the customer for shipping (free + shipping funnel) on the frontend, and then offering upsells after they enter their credit card information such as an online course, membership program, group coaching, or one-on-one session.

10. **Become an expert contributor by writing articles for websites and online magazines in your area of expertise.** This can be done on various sites such as

Medium, Entrepreneur, and Addicted2Success, to name a few. One tip for finding sites in which to contribute is to do a Google search for your main topic plus the words "write for us." For example, a Google search for "Self-publishing write for us" will pull up sites I could write for, and take me directly to their submission guidelines—which, by the way, you'll want to review carefully before you pitch or submit!

11. **Blog on your own website.** Creating content for your own blog is a great way to keep fresh eyes on your website where visitors can ultimately find out about your book and other products and services. Be sure to also share a link to each post across your social media platforms. You never know when one of your articles will get shared or go viral.

12. **Microblog on social media.** Nowadays it's not uncommon to see shorter blog posts being created on social media instead of on the author's website. You see this commonly on Instagram and Facebook, and if you post to Instagram first you have the option to have it shared to Facebook as well so you can essentially kill two birds with one stone. LinkedIn is also a great place to publish articles and showcase your expertise.

13. **Expand your authority through YouTube.** Create a YouTube channel and publish regular video content as the expert in your field by sharing tips, personal experiences, and case studies from your clients' success.

14. **Host your own podcast.** What better way, besides becoming an author, of course, to share your knowledge and grow your following than by hosting a podcast of

your own? As with anything, if you go this route, you'll want to hire someone to help you or take a course to learn how to do it right.

15. **Nurture and grow your mailing list.** You should begin growing your mailing list well in advance of your book's launch, but that doesn't mean you abandon it once your book is published. If you followed the steps in this book, then your book should be a lead-generating machine for your business. Continue to offer value, as you'll hopefully have new subscribers opting in as they find your book, since of course, it will include your awesome bonus gift.

16. **Connect inside your Facebook group.** Be sure to have a Facebook group centralized around your main topic, and show up as the expert by offering value and support. This is an excellent way for you to earn your readers' trust and continue to establish authority in your niche. Have a pinned welcome post that leads new members to your book, sales funnel, and other products and services.

17. **Create a book club for your readers.** If your book walks your reader through a process that can be broken down over time, consider starting a book club so members can work through a chapter each week or month, and then meet for discussion either in person or virtually. Once the curriculum is laid out, encourage others to start their own book club with your book as the focus. You can also start a group on Meetup.com, where it will be listed under various categories.

18. **Create an online course.** Creating an online course to complement your book not only allows your readers to

dive deeper into your content, it can be an awesome upsell for your book funnel or call-to-action page for backend sales. It's easy to turn the topic from each chapter into its own module and expand upon the content by including video tutorials, worksheets, checklists, and templates. Your book should offer plenty of value on its own, and your course should be a deeper dive into the topic while walking your student step-by-step through the process.

19. **Include group coaching or a mastermind.** Your course on its own can be evergreen (enroll anytime; work-at-your-own-pace), but for a more premium offer and perhaps an additional upsell, consider adding a live element by offering group coaching or a mastermind for those who are ready to take it to the next level with you as their mentor.

20. **Offer one-on-one mentoring or a done-for-you service.** Private coaching is usually a premium offer (your time is valuable, isn't it?) but it's often the next logical step after someone has read your book, taken your program, and wants to continue the journey with you with more focused attention. One of my mentors, Sunny Dawn Johnston, once told me: *Some people have more time than money, but others have more money than time.* While it's nice to offer people a way to learn to do something for themselves, don't forget to create an offer for those who would rather just pay you to do it for them. That's why at the back of this book you'll notice I cater to both audiences: I have a link for my flagship program, the Author Success Academy, but I also offer my Deluxe Bestselling Author Program—my done-for-you service that takes you

from manuscript to bestselling author, with me as your personal coach and project manager.

21. **Host a retreat or live workshop.** I usually try to host either an annual or biannual retreat, and nowadays, it's not uncommon for these to take place online. Either find an enticing location where everyone can come together and connect in person, or offer it virtually through Zoom. You can even create virtual breakout rooms through Zoom to promote close connections between attendees.

22. **Run discounted quarterly promotions on your Kindle edition.** As mentioned, once your keywords and categories are optimized during your launch, it's a good idea to run quarterly promotions by dropping the price of the e-book to free or $.99 every few months and scheduling some paid features with book promoters. This will give your sales ranking a boost, get new readers for your book, and grow your list since your book includes an awesome free gift inside.

23. **Write more books and create a series.** Book series do great via Amazon and other online retailers, so continue to share your expertise in a variety of ways and connect them together in a series. Be sure to promote the other books in your series at the back of each book, and create a series page on Amazon through your KDP account so that Amazon will feature the other books in your series on each book's product page. The more books you write, the more your authority and credibility will grow, and the more opportunities you'll have to attract your target audience into your world where you'll continue to nurture them and ultimately turn them into clients.

The goal is to always look for ways to share your message and your expertise with the world, and allow your ideal reader various avenues and opportunities to connect with you and run across your book. Once they look to you as an expert, they will seek to learn more and ultimately find your book, along with your other products and services.

In Closing

I'd like to thank you for taking this journey with me as I opened up about my own process that I use to help authors write, publish and launch bestselling books that not only make an impact on their readers but their own lives and businesses as well.

By now you should know exactly what to include in your book to ensure it speaks to your ideal reader *and* sets you up for long-term success as an author. My hope is that you are looking at authorship as a way to grow your credibility and authority, and expand your message beyond the book through backend offers—where the real income for authors is made.

I hope by now you have a better understanding of the self-publishing process, at least from my perspective. Know that there are many paths to success and only you can decide which one is right for you; therefore, I always recommend that you do your own research as well. Should you have questions along the way, please know help is always available to you, and I outline different ways we can connect or work together in the following section.

If I may leave you with one closing thought, it is this: please remember that authorship is not a one-and-done type of thing, and it shouldn't be rushed just to get your book out faster. Look at it as an extension of yourself and your brand, and an investment in your future. Take the time to structure your book in a way that will help you deliver valuable content that could stand on its own, but also turn your readers into subscribers and possibly even clients. Invest in the things that will allow you to create a high-quality book that doesn't appear self-published, as that's the key to successful self-publishing, after all.

And finally, once your book is out in the world, don't just launch it and then let the momentum die. Always continue to find clever ways to keep your book in front of your target audience, and in turn, it will continue to attract and funnel new readers and even clients into your business for many years to come.

My wish was to write this book so you could avoid the mistakes I see so many first-time authors make, so you can do it right straight out of the gate and birth a book that you're proud to share with the world—one that lends you authority and credibility, and impacts the lives of your readers.

Now it's time for you to take what you've learned here and get started, or even relaunch a second edition of a book that's already been published.

You've got this!

To your success,
Shanda

How to Get More Help

Throughout this book I've talked to you about the importance of your call-to-action page. Well, here is mine. Not every reader, but most, who get to the back of your book may be interested in working with you further or at least joining your mailing list, community, and consuming additional content. If that's you, I want to offer you a variety of options:

Self-Publishing Success Checklist: If you haven't downloaded it yet, don't miss out on your free three-part checklist to keep you on track through the production, launch, and post-launch marketing process. Download it here:

shandatrofe.com/checklist

Author Coaching: Whether you're seeking an immersive VIP experience, personalized voice/text coaching, or the support of my flagship group coaching program, my services are tailored to meet you exactly where you are on your authorship journey. Visit:

shandatrofe.com/coaching

Deluxe Bestselling Author Package: This premium offer is perfect for aspiring authors who want to avoid navigating the complexities of self-publishing on their own. Instead, you can partner with me and my expert team at Transcendent Publishing to create a high-quality, bestselling book and launch it to the world with professionalism and impact. As your dedicated project manager and coach, I'll guide you every step of the way, ensuring a seamless and successful publishing journey. If you're ready to work with me and my team at Transcendent Publishing, apply here:

workwithshanda.com

Acknowledgments

First and foremost, I'd like to thank my past clients and students. Without you, I wouldn't have learned what works, what doesn't, and what questions first-time authors are plagued with throughout their authorship journey. YOU are all the reason why I do what I do, and I hope I've done right by you through my endless need to stay up on what's trending and what's most effective in making your path to success as smooth and easy as possible.

I'd like to thank my design team at Transcendent Publishing for working tirelessly throughout the year for our clients, but also squeezing in the final touches on this project over the holiday break. I'm blessed with an amazing team, and I'm beyond grateful to have each and every one of you.

Especially Dana, my go-to editor and the behind-the-scenes hero to so many of my authors. I'm always in awe at the number of books you're able to edit in a year's time, and I'm grateful anytime you edit and polish my work as you always have a way to make my writing so much stronger. You're not only an angel in my life, but to so many of my clients. Thank you for all that you do.

And finally, to my mentors: Sunny Dawn Johnston for being a living and breathing example of a true authorpreneur, and trusting me with all of your self-published books. And to Russell Brunson and Dan Henry for showing me the power of a book funnel, and writing and creating a high-quality book that delivers insane value but also grows your business.